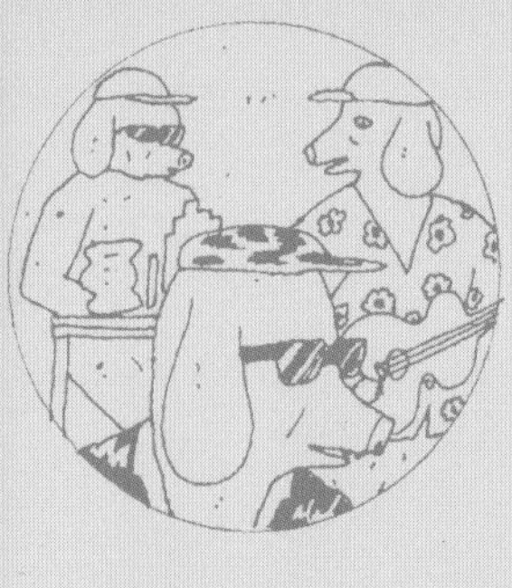

JEFF ZONE

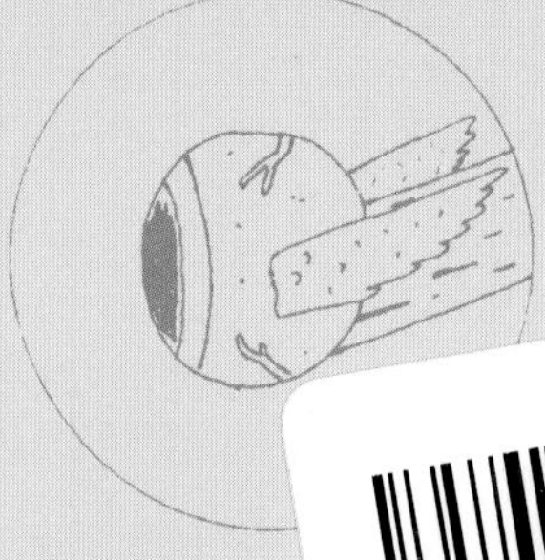

THE GU

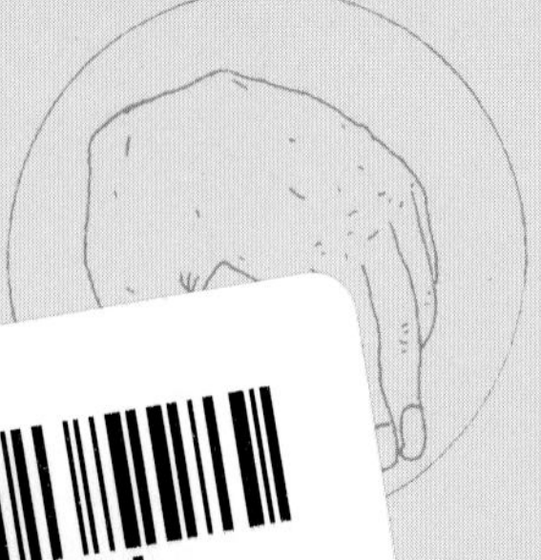

DESTINY

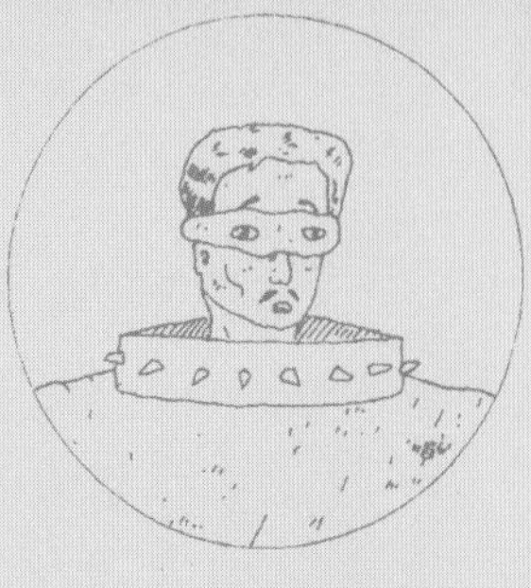

CAPTAIN LITTLEHEAD

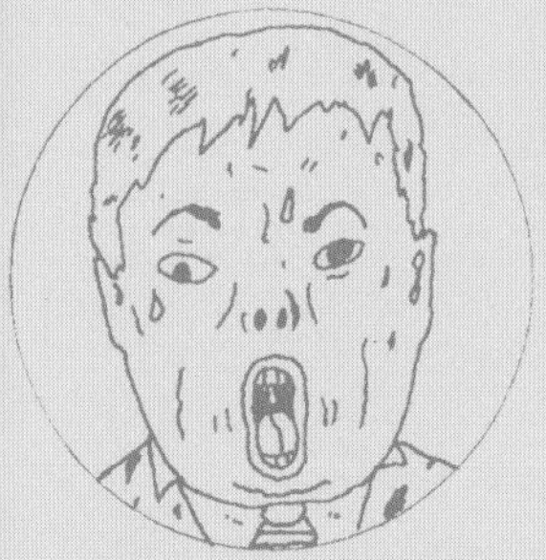

B. FLUMP

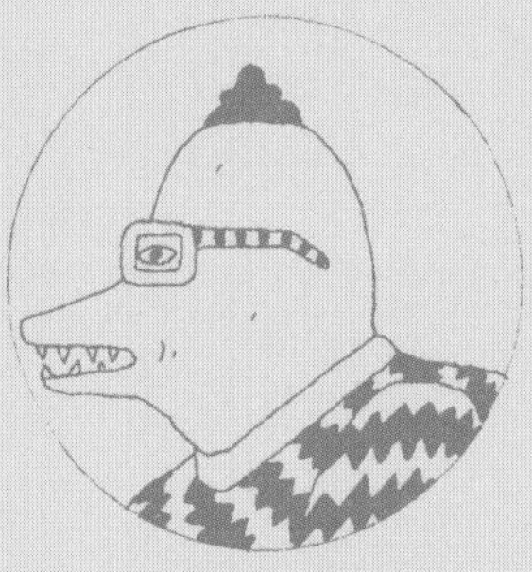

GUEST 2

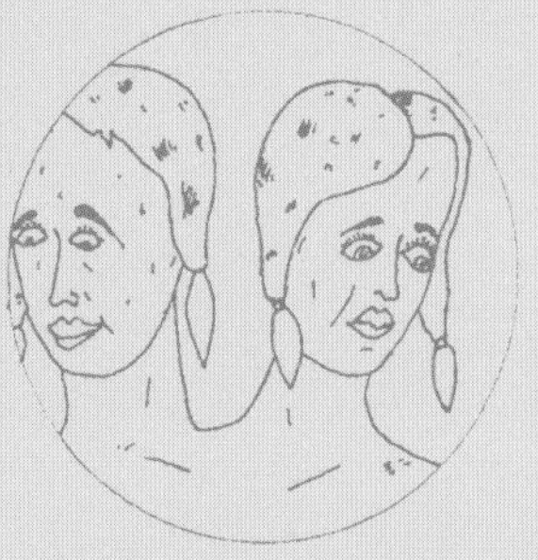

ENTERTAINERS

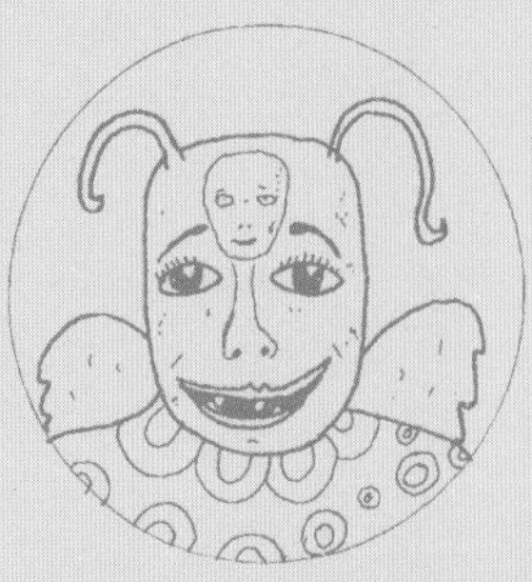

THE HERMANS

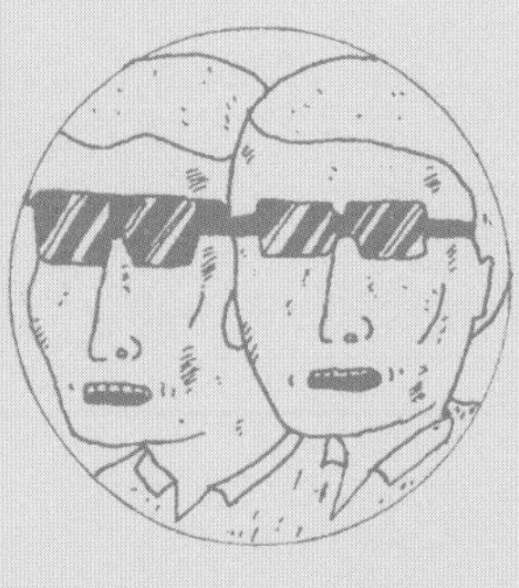

THE ONLOOKERS

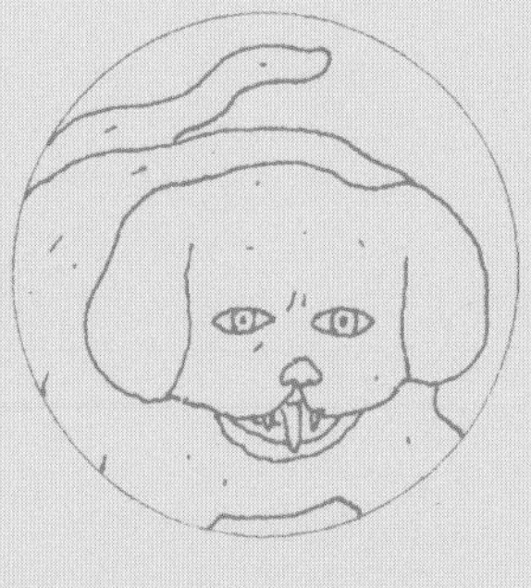

CHESWICK

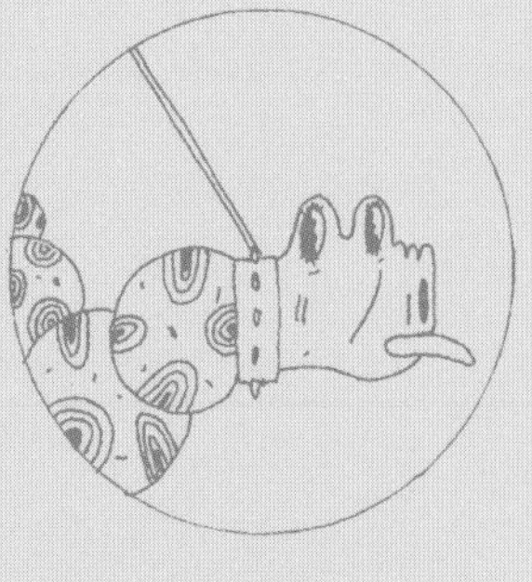

SNAGGLE WORM

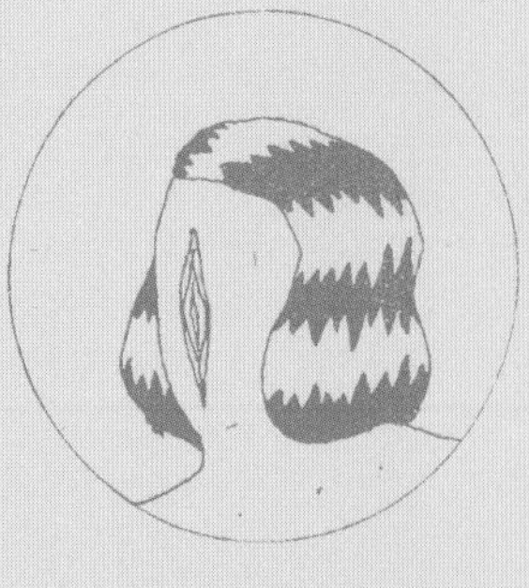

ENTERTAINER 3

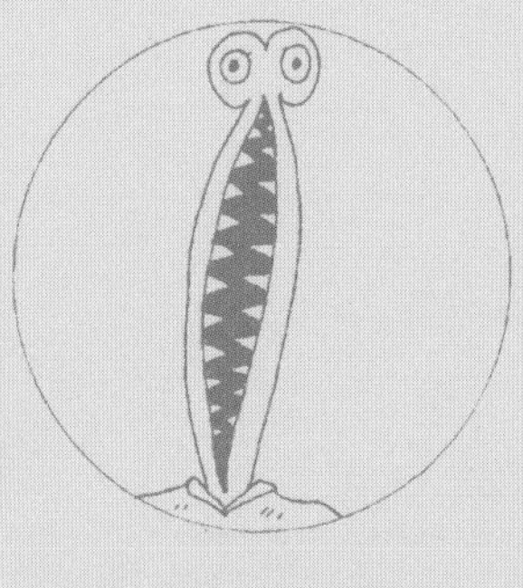

GUEST 4

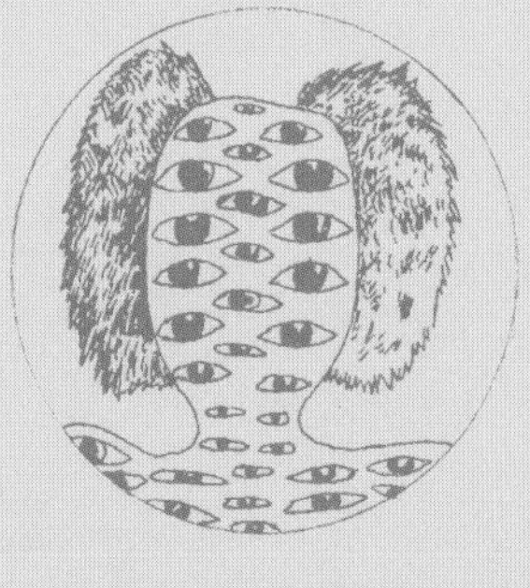

THE SECRETARY

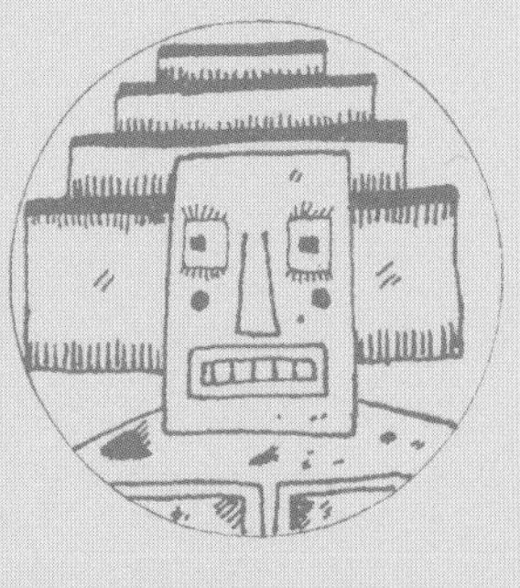

ENTERTAINER 4

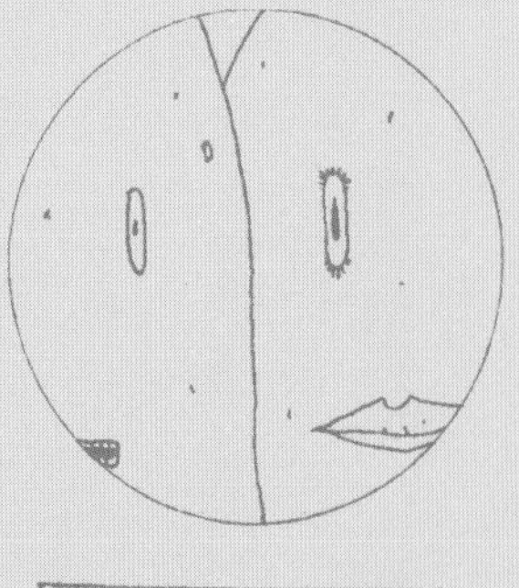

GUESTS 5+6

MOTEL UNIVERSE
BY JOAKIM DRESCHER

SECRET
ACRES

Motel Universe © Joakim Drescher 2019.

First edition.

Printed in China.

ISBN-13: 978-0-9991935-3-2
ISBN-10: 0-9991935-3-8

SA041

Library of Congress Control Number:
2018958136

Published by Secret Acres
200 Park Avenue South, 8th fl.

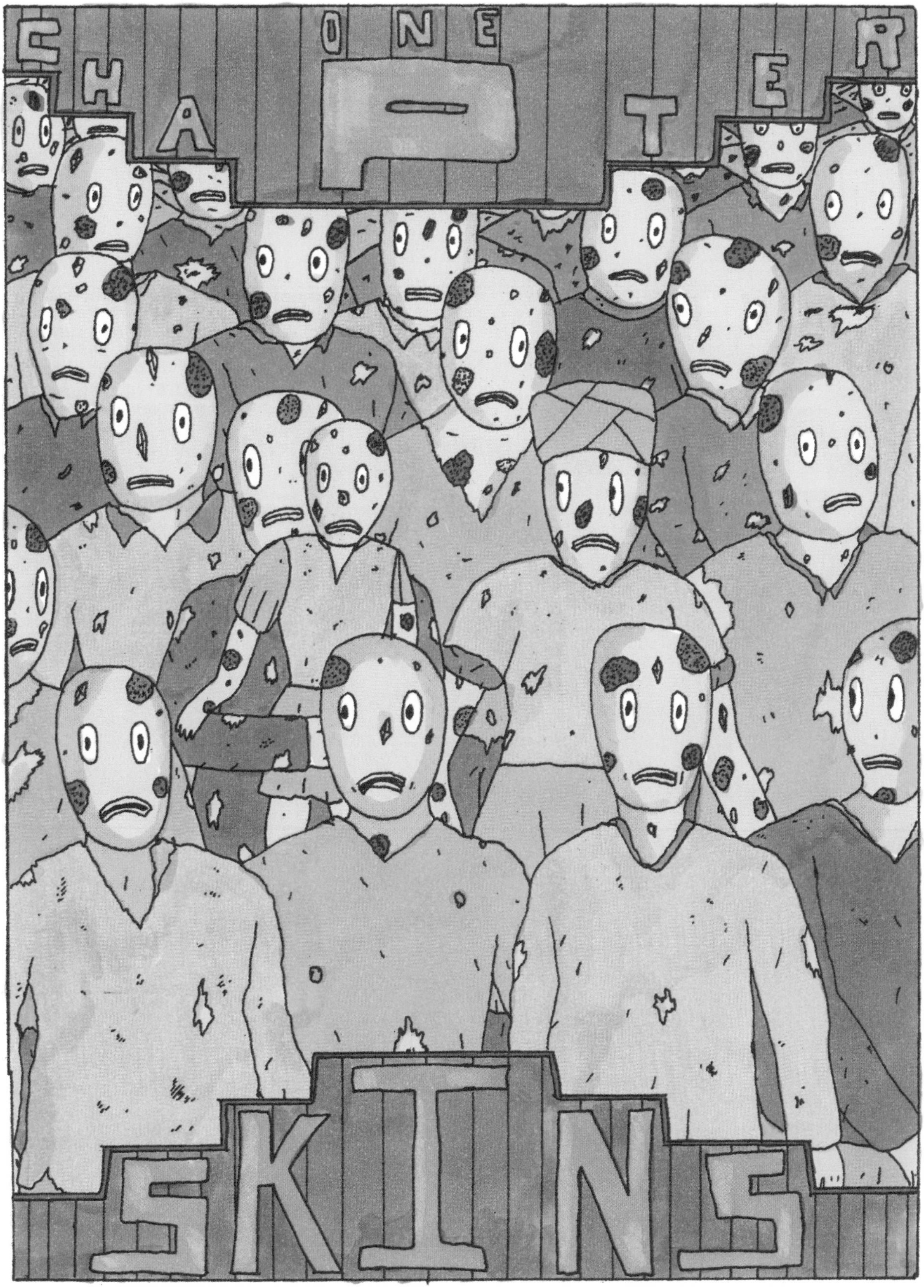
CHAPTER
ONE
SKINS

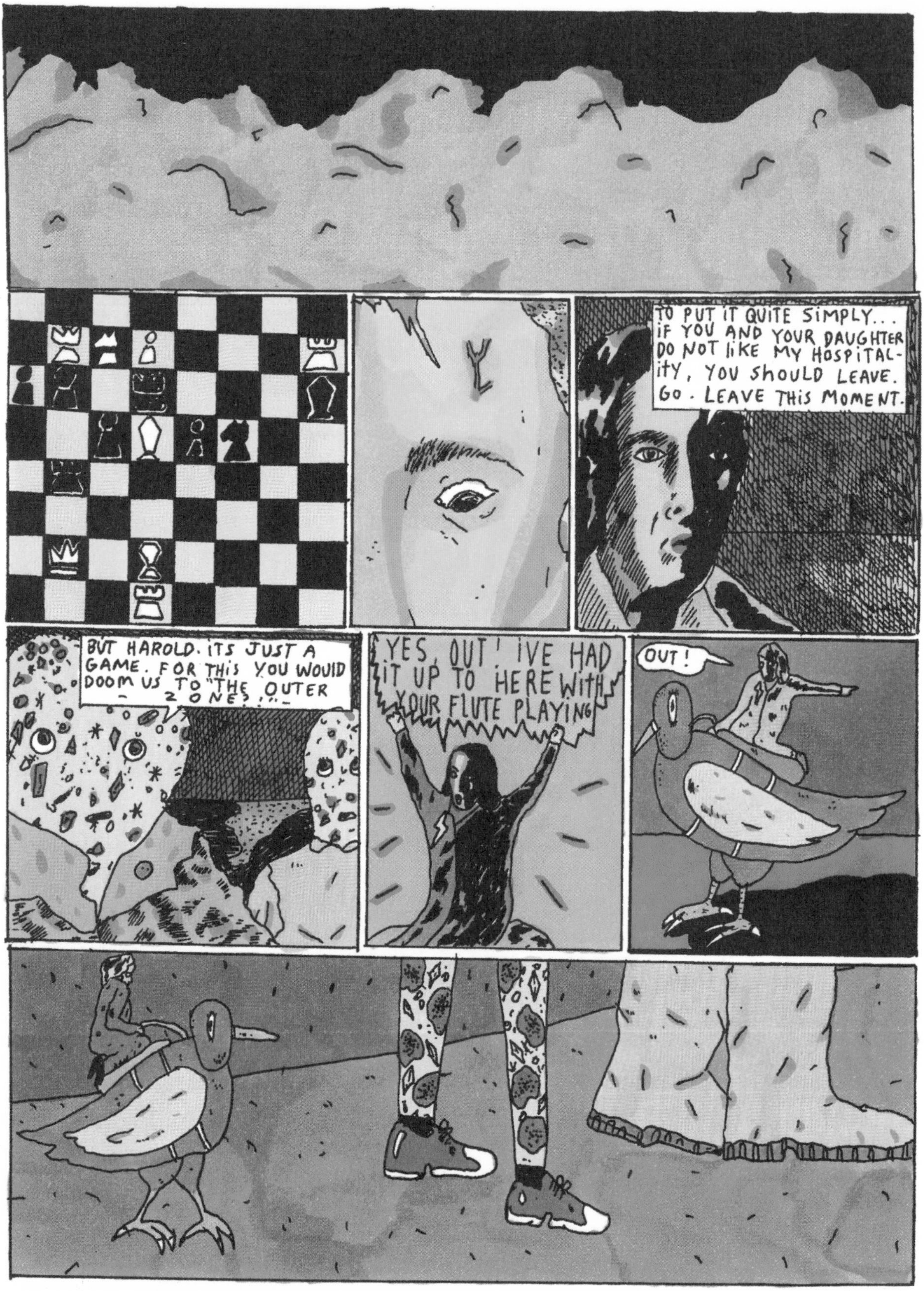

TO PUT IT QUITE SIMPLY... IF YOU AND YOUR DAUGHTER DO NOT LIKE MY HOSPITAL-ITY, YOU SHOULD LEAVE. GO. LEAVE THIS MOMENT.
BUT HAROLD. ITS JUST A GAME. FOR THIS YOU WOULD DOOM US TO "THE OUTER ZONES!"
YES, OUT! IVE HAD IT UP TO HERE WITH YOUR FLUTE PLAYING
OUT!

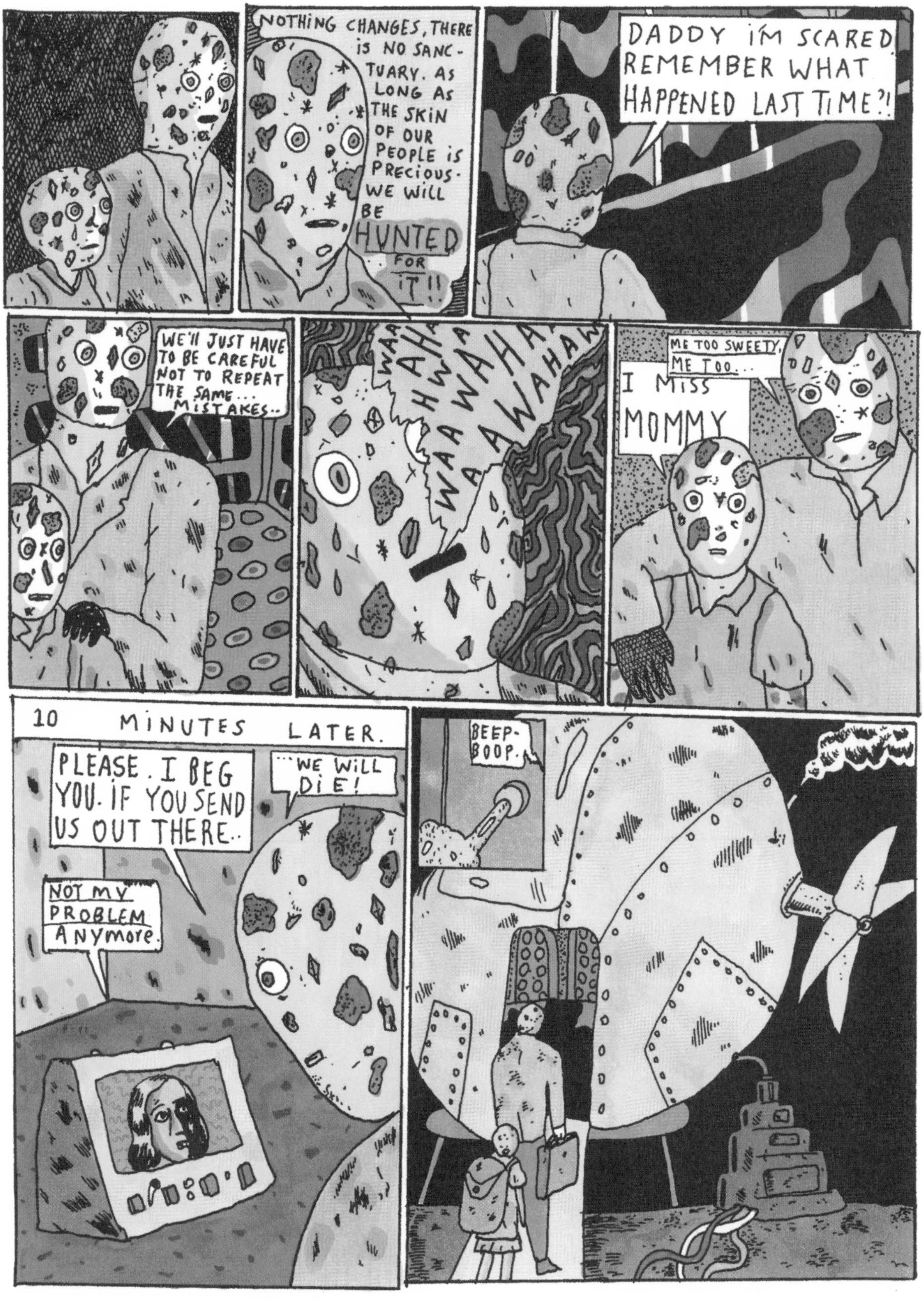
NOTHING CHANGES, THERE IS NO SANCTUARY. AS LONG AS THE SKIN OF OUR PEOPLE IS PRECIOUS- WE WILL BE HUNTED FOR IT!!
DADDY I'M SCARED REMEMBER WHAT HAPPENED LAST TIME?!
WE'LL JUST HAVE TO BE CAREFUL NOT TO REPEAT THE SAME... MISTAKES..
WAA AHA WAA WAHAHA WAA WAHAW
I MISS MOMMY
ME TOO SWEETY, ME TOO...
10 MINUTES LATER.
PLEASE. I BEG YOU. IF YOU SEND US OUT THERE..
...WE WILL DIE!
NOT MY PROBLEM Anymore.
BEEP-BOOP.

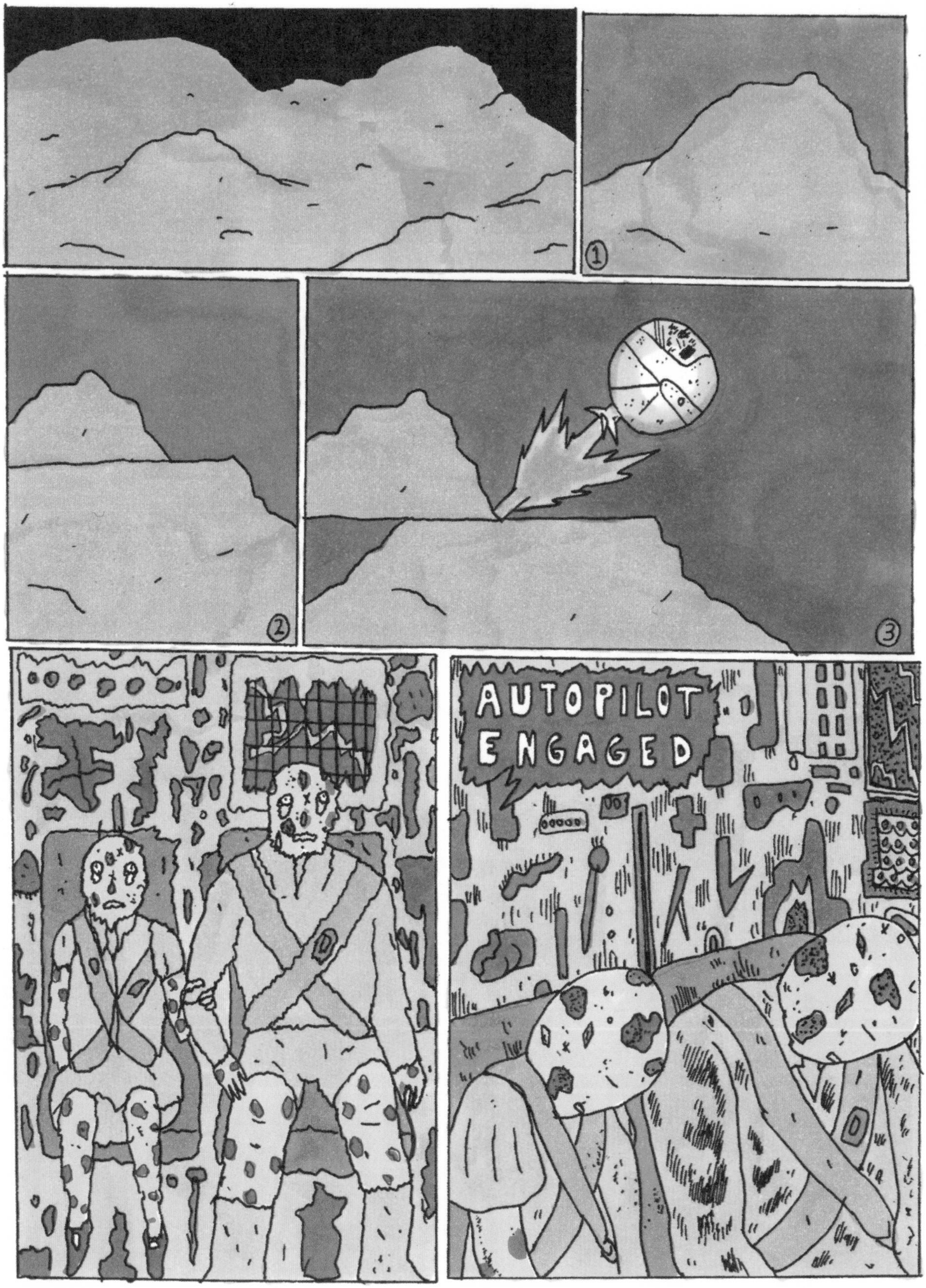
1
2
3
AUTOPILOT ENGAGED

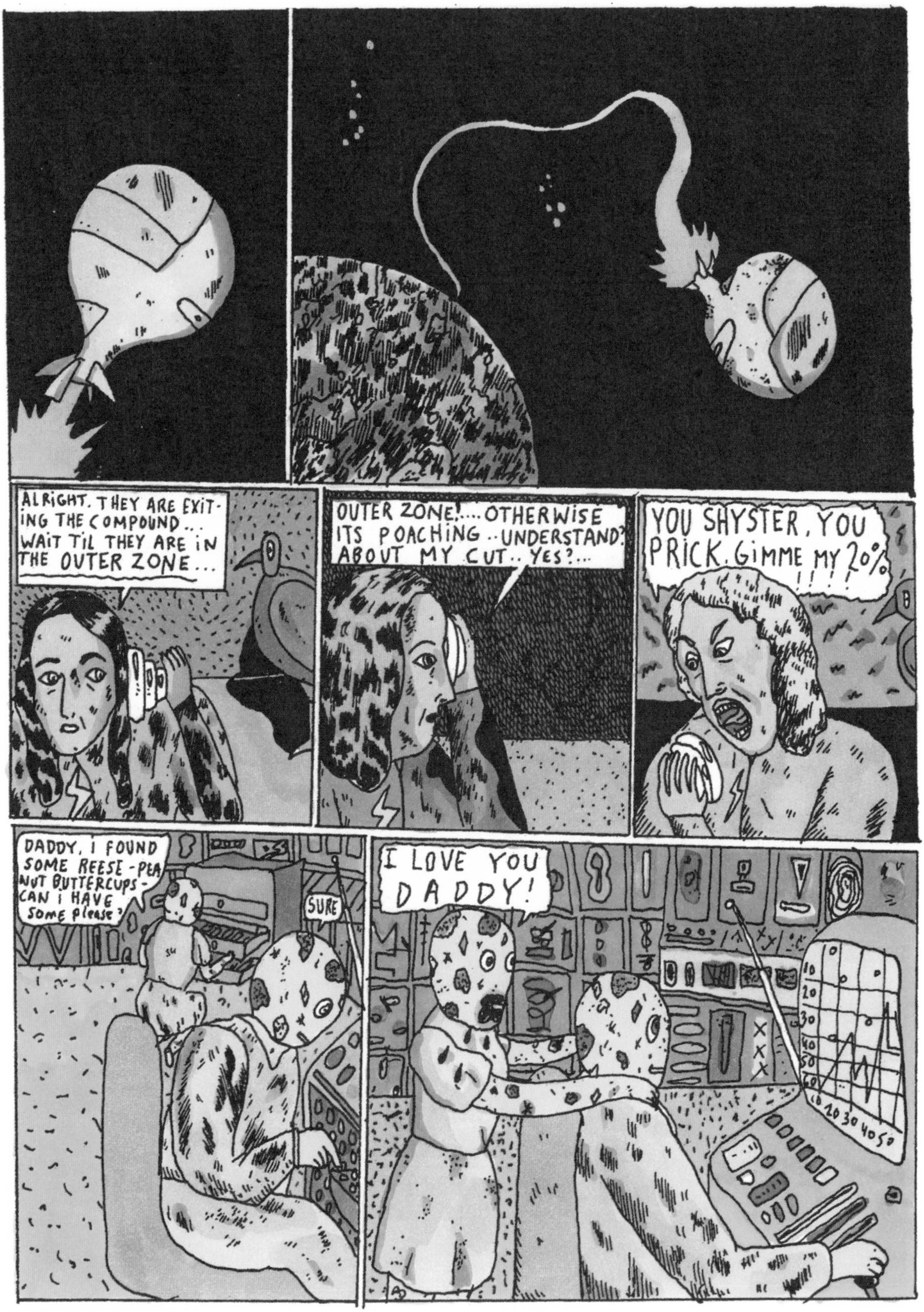
ALRIGHT. THEY ARE EXITING THE COMPOUND... WAIT TIL THEY ARE IN THE OUTER ZONE...
OUTER ZONE!.... OTHERWISE ITS POACHING .. UNDERSTAND? ABOUT MY CUT.. YES?...
YOU SHYSTER, YOU PRICK. GIMME MY 20% !!!!!
DADDY, I FOUND SOME REESE-PEANUT BUTTERCUPS - CAN I HAVE SOME please?
SURE
I LOVE YOU DADDY!

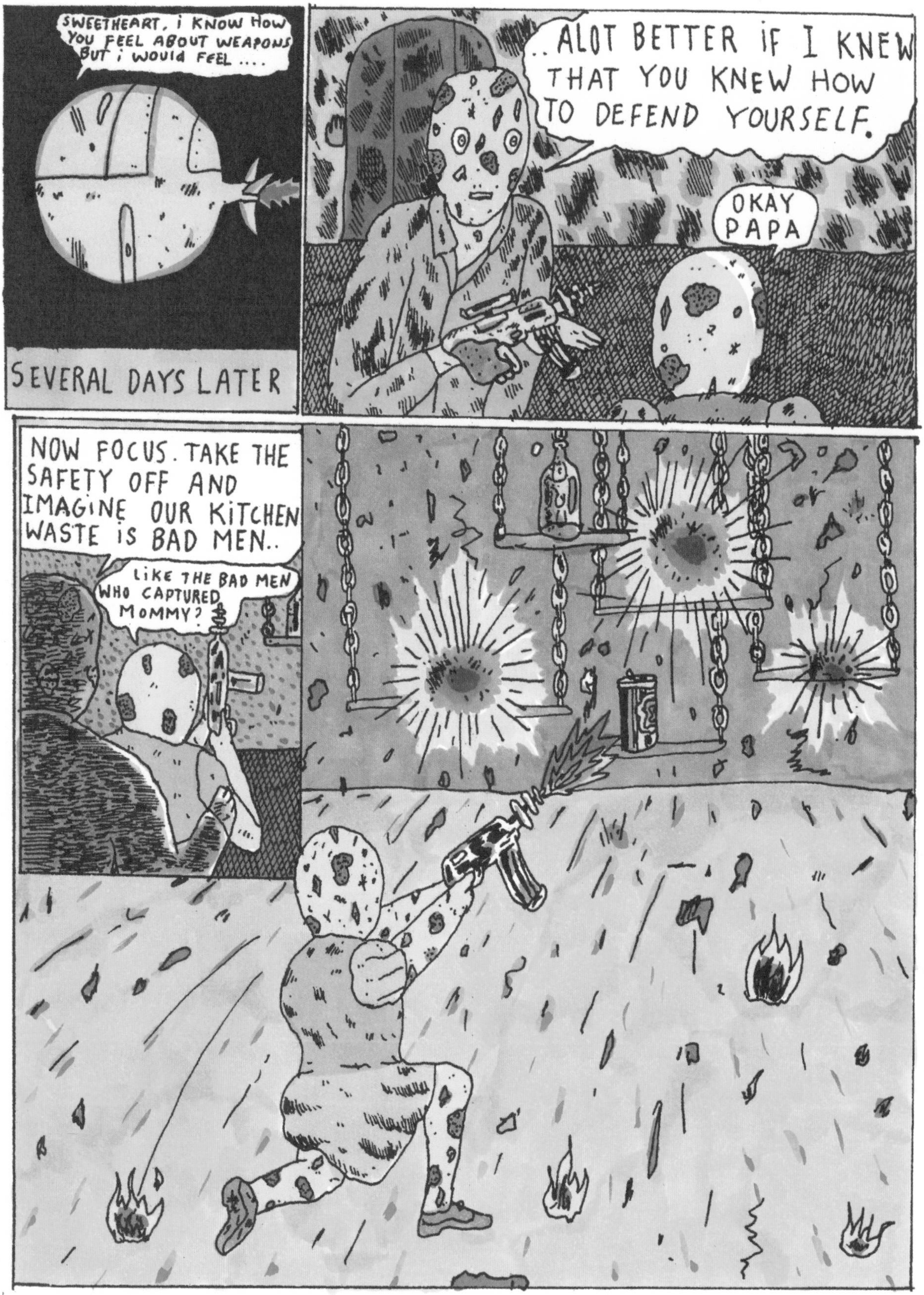
SWEETHEART, i KNOW HOW YOU FEEL ABOUT WEAPONS BUT i WOULD FEEL ....
SEVERAL DAYS LATER
..ALOT BETTER iF I KNEW THAT YOU KNEW HOW TO DEFEND YOURSELF.
OKAY PAPA
NOW FOCUS. TAKE THE SAFETY OFF AND IMAGINE OUR KITCHEN WASTE IS BAD MEN..
LIKE THE BAD MEN WHO CAPTURED MOMMY?

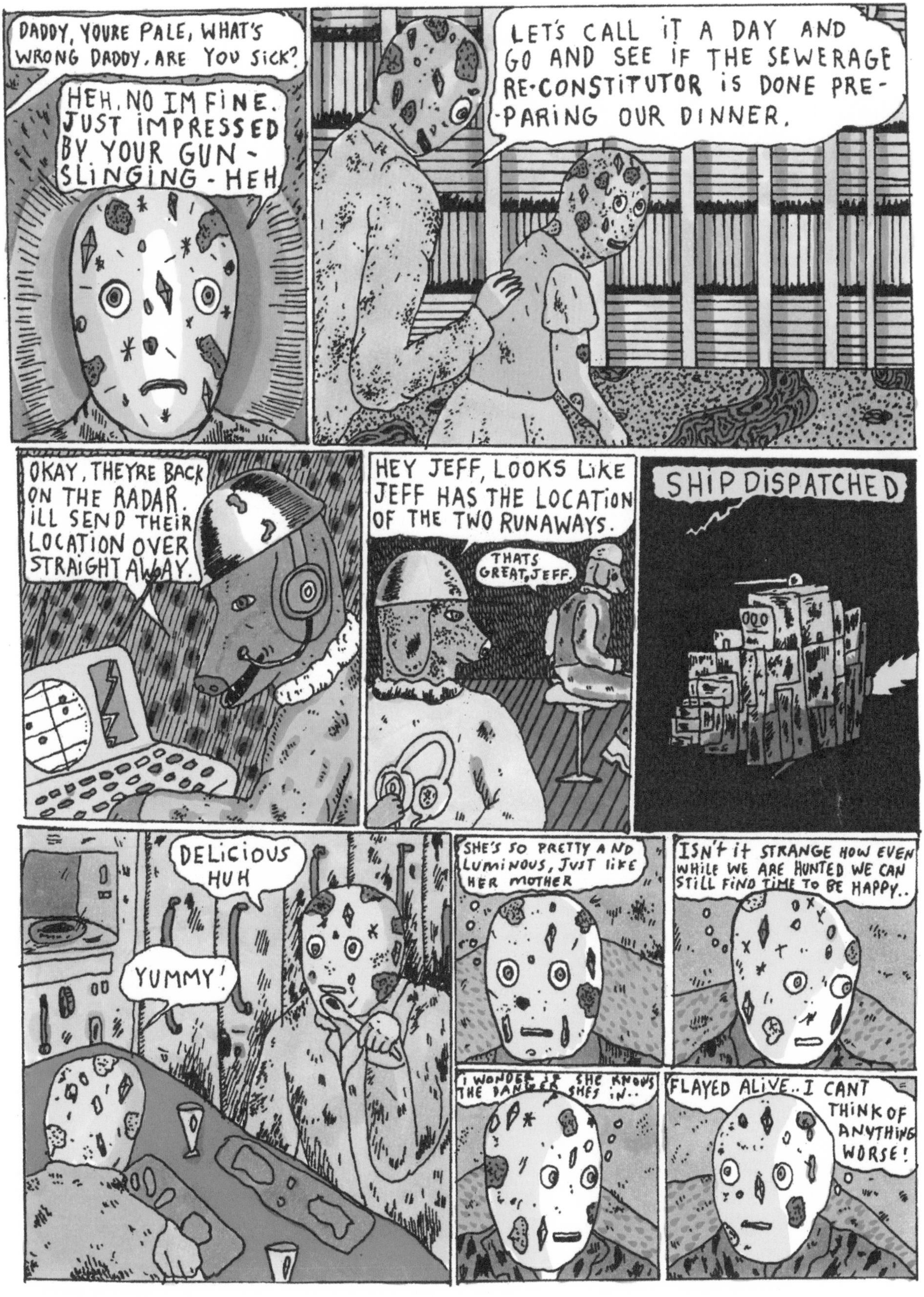
DADDY, YOURE PALE, WHAT'S WRONG DADDY, ARE YOU SICK?
HEH, NO IM FINE. JUST IMPRESSED BY YOUR GUN-SLINGING - HEH
LET'S CALL IT A DAY AND GO AND SEE IF THE SEWERAGE RE-CONSTITUTOR IS DONE PRE-PARING OUR DINNER.
OKAY, THEYRE BACK ON THE RADAR. ILL SEND THEIR LOCATION OVER STRAIGHT AWAY.
HEY JEFF, LOOKS LIKE JEFF HAS THE LOCATION OF THE TWO RUNAWAYS.
THATS GREAT, JEFF.
SHIP DISPATCHED
DELICIOUS HUH
YUMMY!
SHE'S SO PRETTY AND LUMINOUS, JUST LIKE HER MOTHER
ISN'T IT STRANGE HOW EVEN WHILE WE ARE HUNTED WE CAN STILL FIND TIME TO BE HAPPY..
I WONDER IF SHE KNOWS THE DANGER SHES IN..
FLAYED ALIVE.. I CANT THINK OF ANYTHING WORSE!

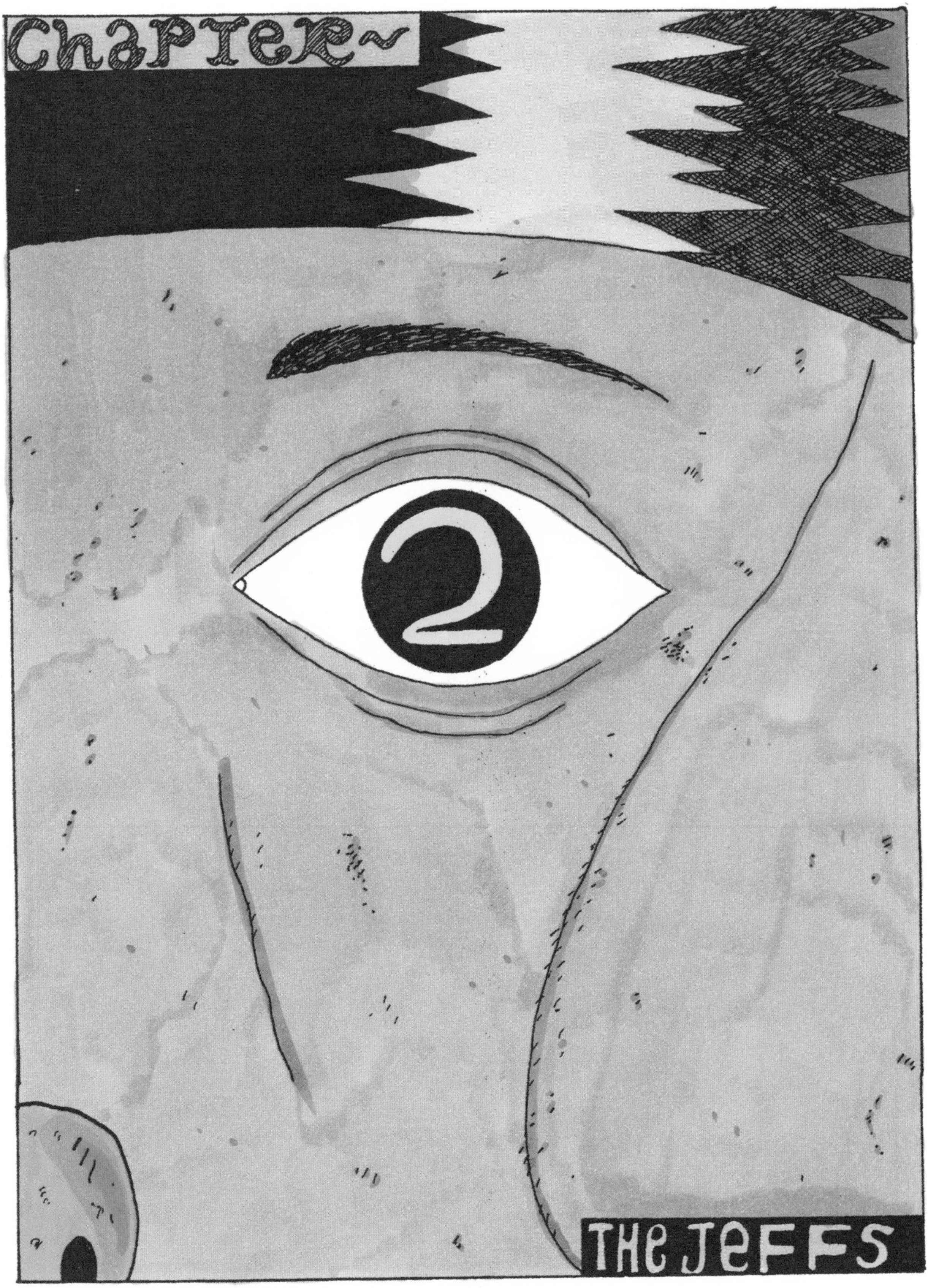

Chapter~
2
The Jeffs

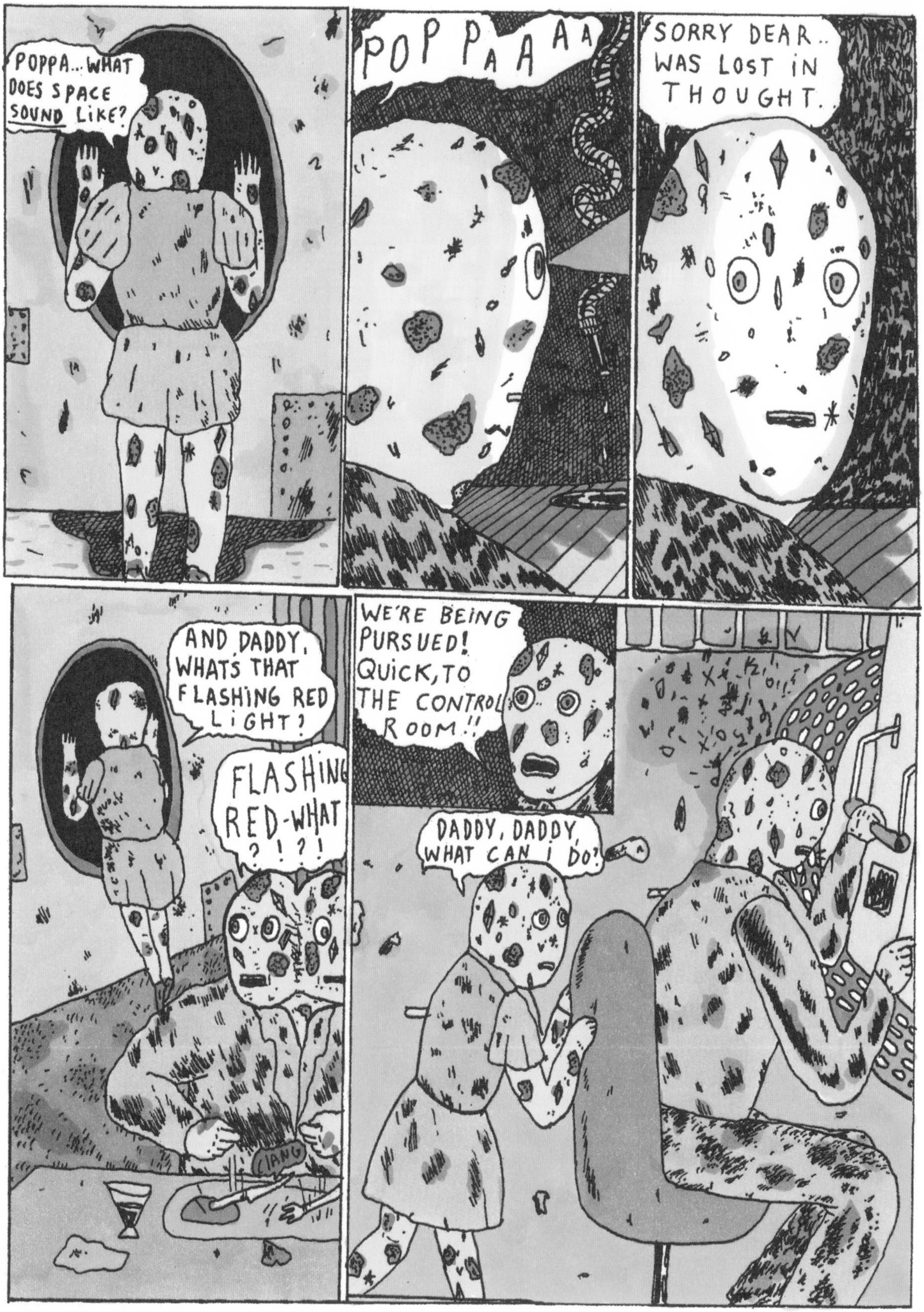
POPPA... WHAT DOES SPACE SOUND LIKE?
POPPAAAA
SORRY DEAR.. WAS LOST IN THOUGHT.
AND DADDY, WHATS THAT FLASHING RED LIGHT?
FLASHING RED-WHAT ?!?!
CLANG
WE'RE BEING PURSUED! QUICK, TO THE CONTROL ROOM!!
DADDY, DADDY, WHAT CAN I DO?

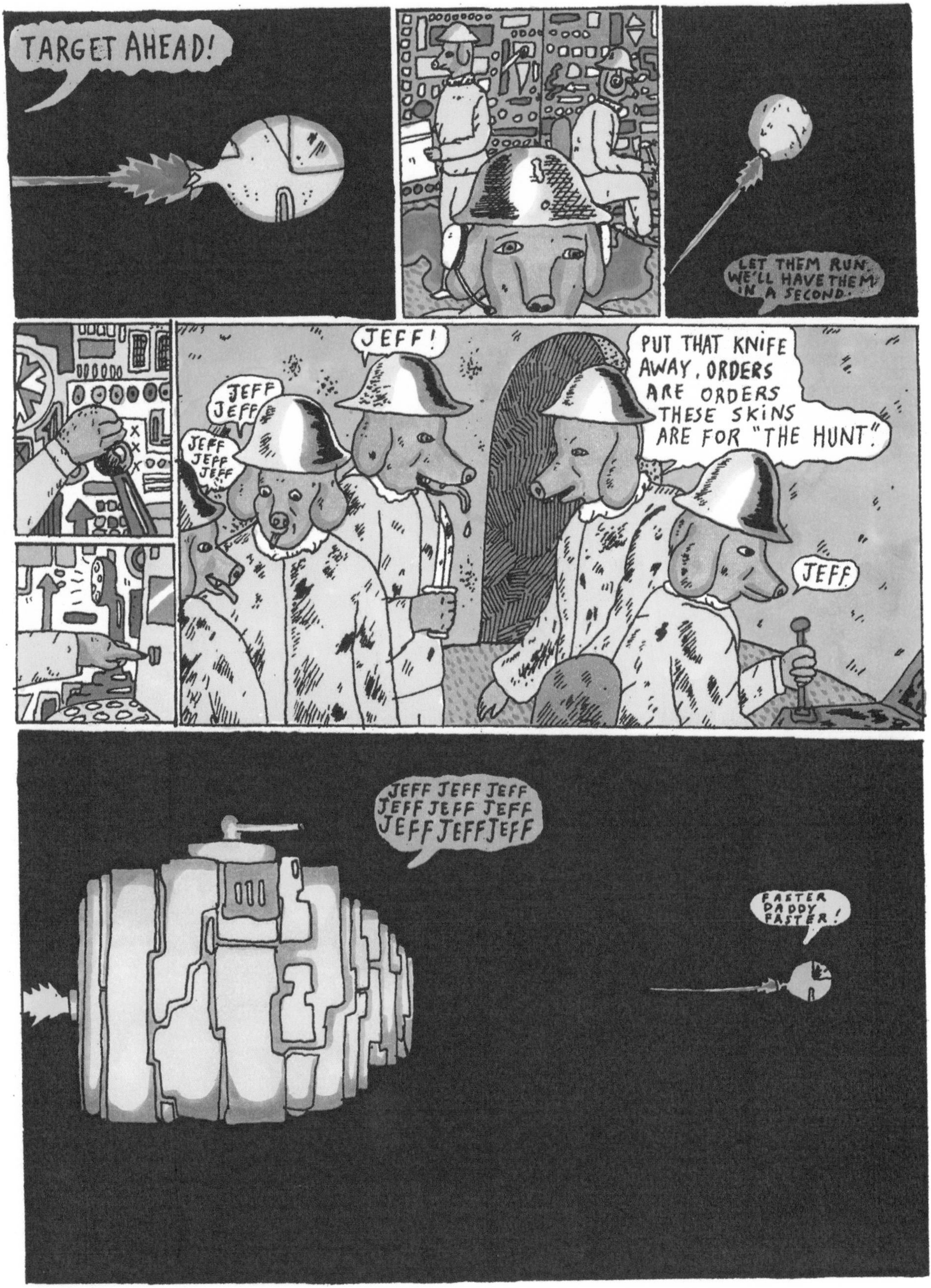
TARGET AHEAD!
LET THEM RUN. WE'LL HAVE THEM IN A SECOND.
JEFF!
JEFF JEFF
JEFF JEFF JEFF
PUT THAT KNIFE AWAY, ORDERS ARE ORDERS THESE SKINS ARE FOR "THE HUNT".
JEFF
JEFF JEFF JEFF JEFF JEFF JEFF JEFF JEFF JEFF
FASTER DADDY FASTER!

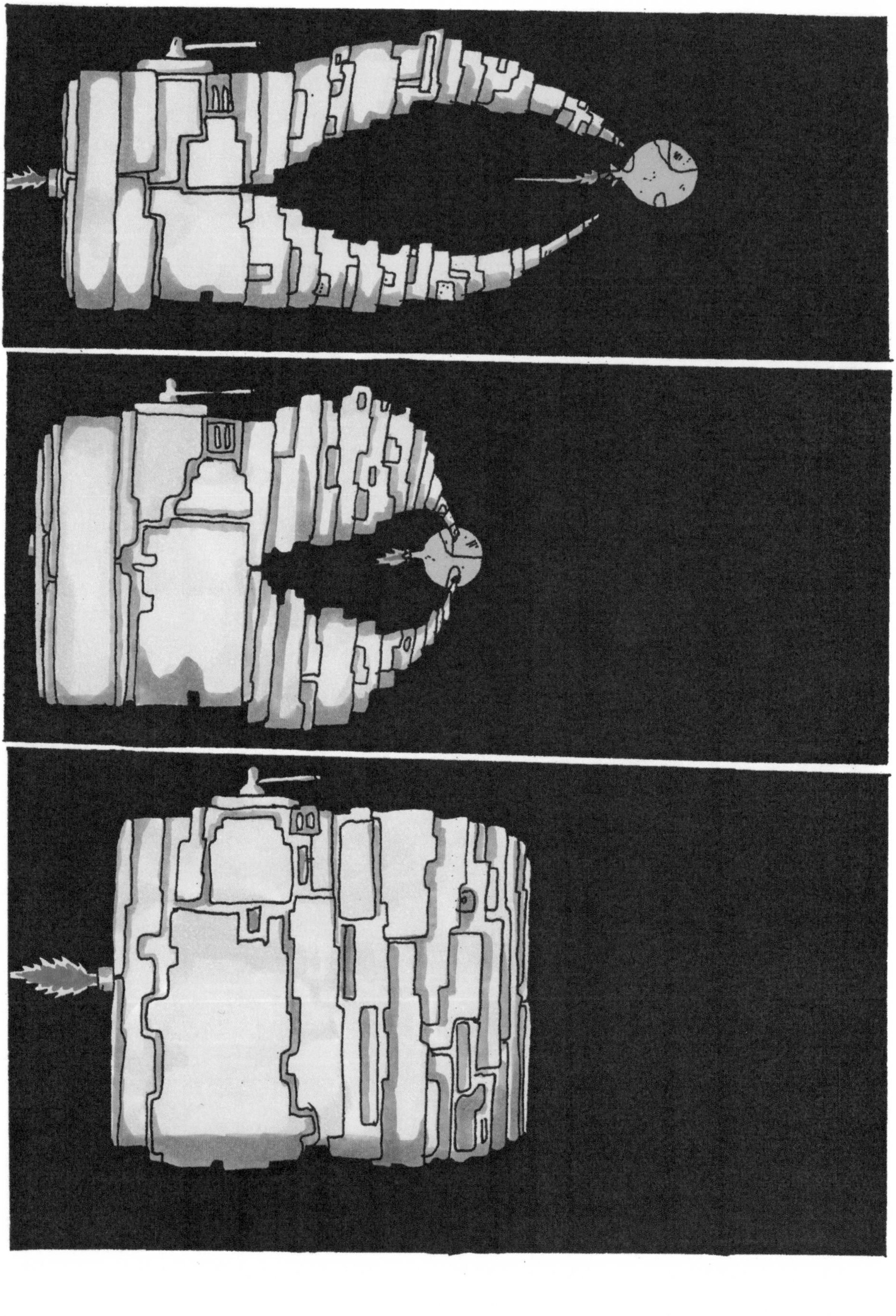

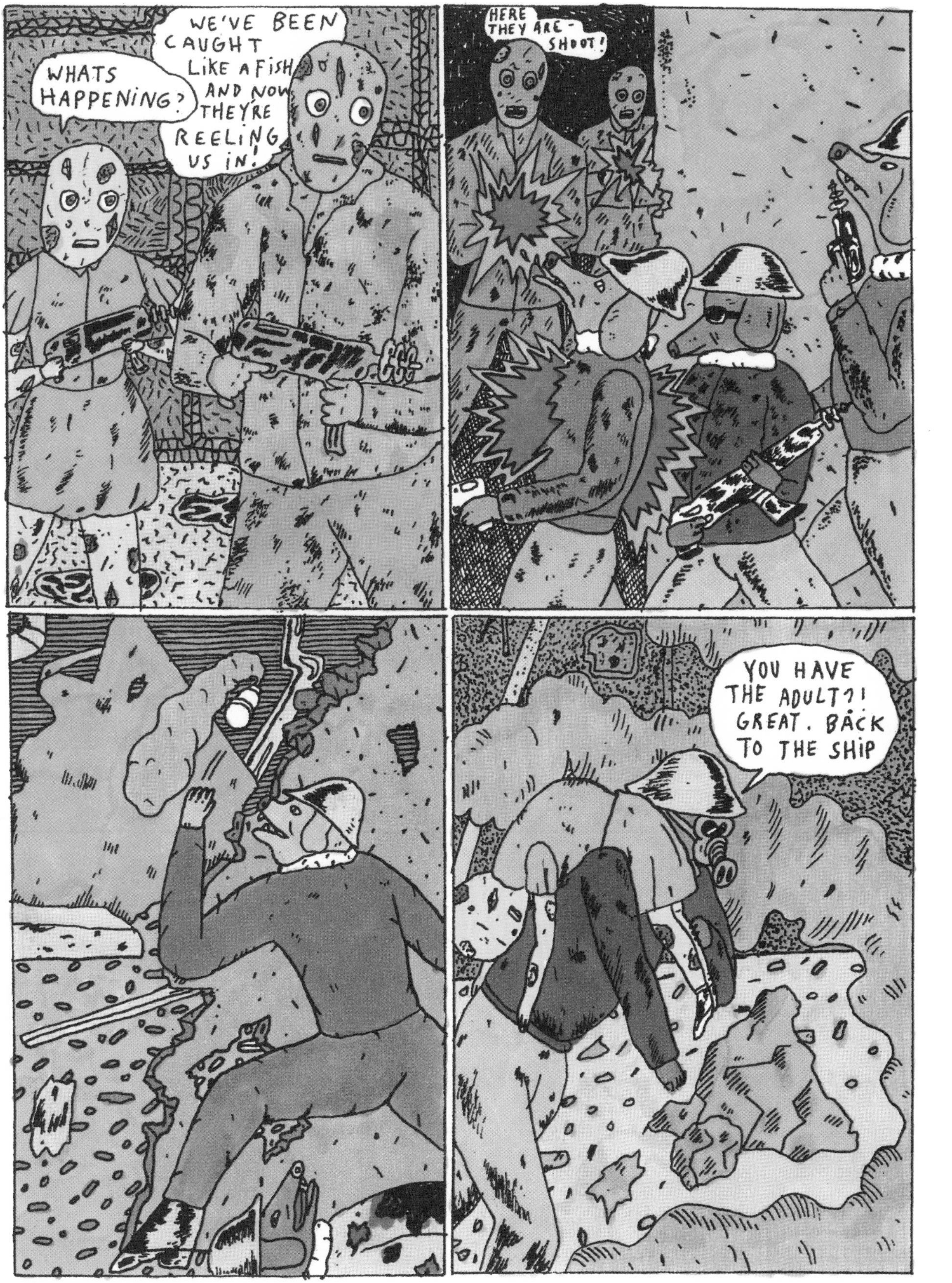
WHATS HAPPENING?
WE'VE BEEN CAUGHT LIKE A FISH AND NOW THEY'RE REELING US IN!
HERE THEY ARE - SHOOT!
YOU HAVE THE ADULT?! GREAT. BACK TO THE SHIP

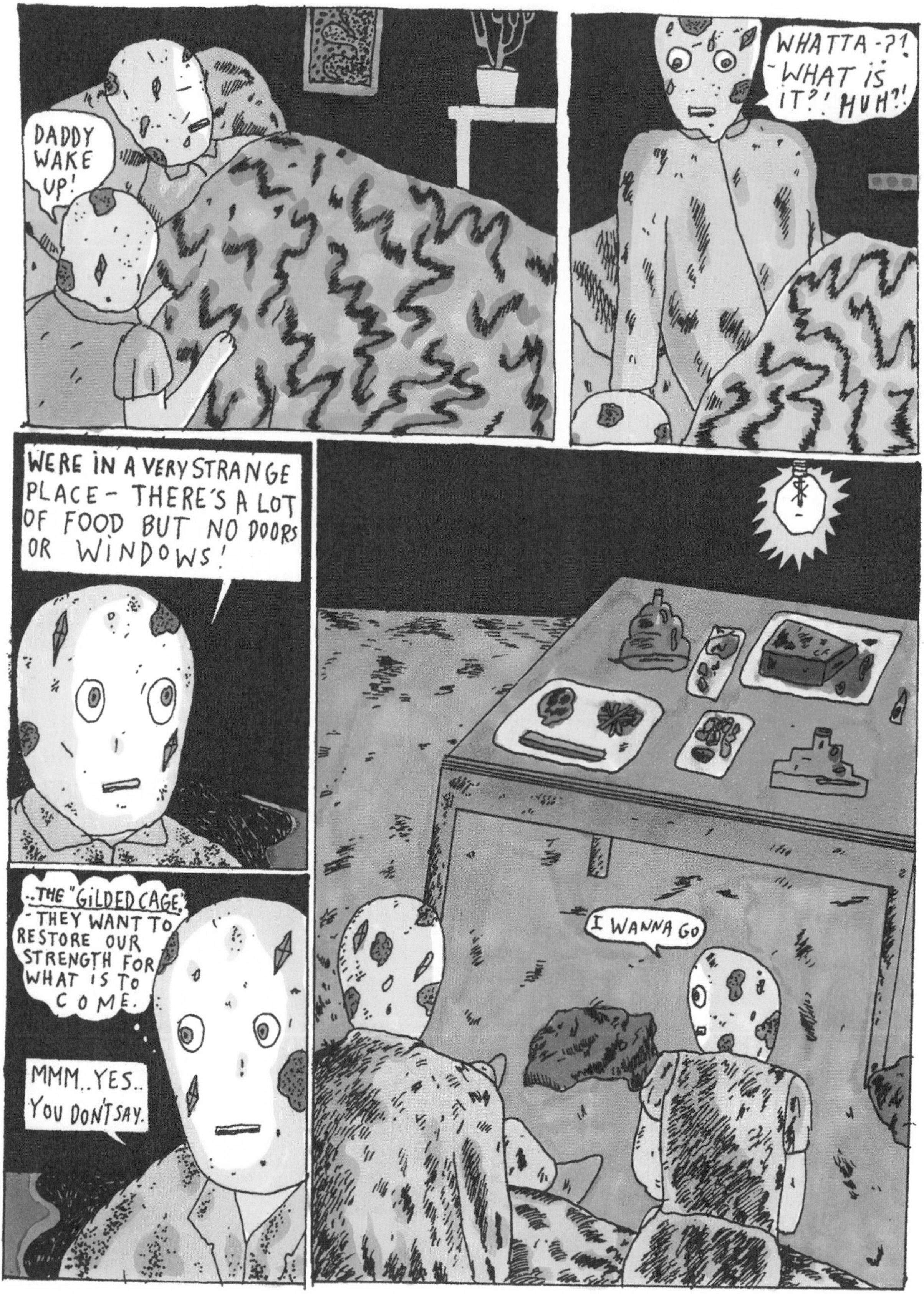
DADDY WAKE UP!
WHATTA -?! -WHAT IS IT?! HUH?!
WERE IN A VERY STRANGE PLACE - THERE'S A LOT OF FOOD BUT NO DOORS OR WINDOWS!
..THE "GILDED CAGE" - THEY WANT TO RESTORE OUR STRENGTH FOR WHAT IS TO COME.
MMM..YES.. YOU DON'T SAY.
I WANNA GO

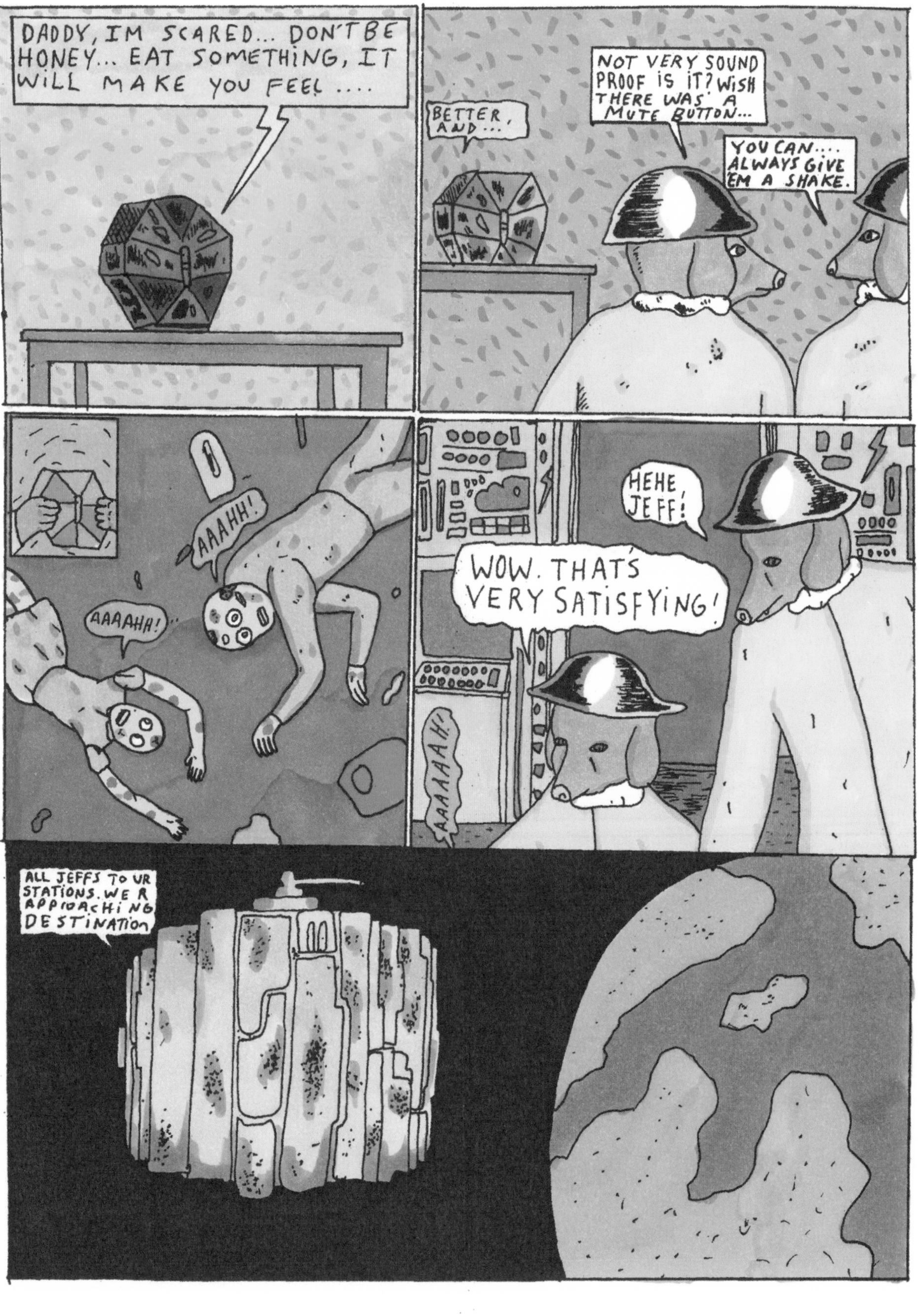
DADDY, IM SCARED... DON'T BE HONEY... EAT SOMETHING, IT WILL MAKE YOU FEEL ....
BETTER, AND....
NOT VERY SOUND PROOF IS IT? WISH THERE WAS A MUTE BUTTON...
YOU CAN.... ALWAYS GIVE 'EM A SHAKE.
AAAHH!
AAAAHH!...
HEHE, JEFF!
WOW. THAT'S VERY SATISFYING!
AAAAAAH!
ALL JEFFS TO UR STATIONS. WE R APPROACHING DESTINATION

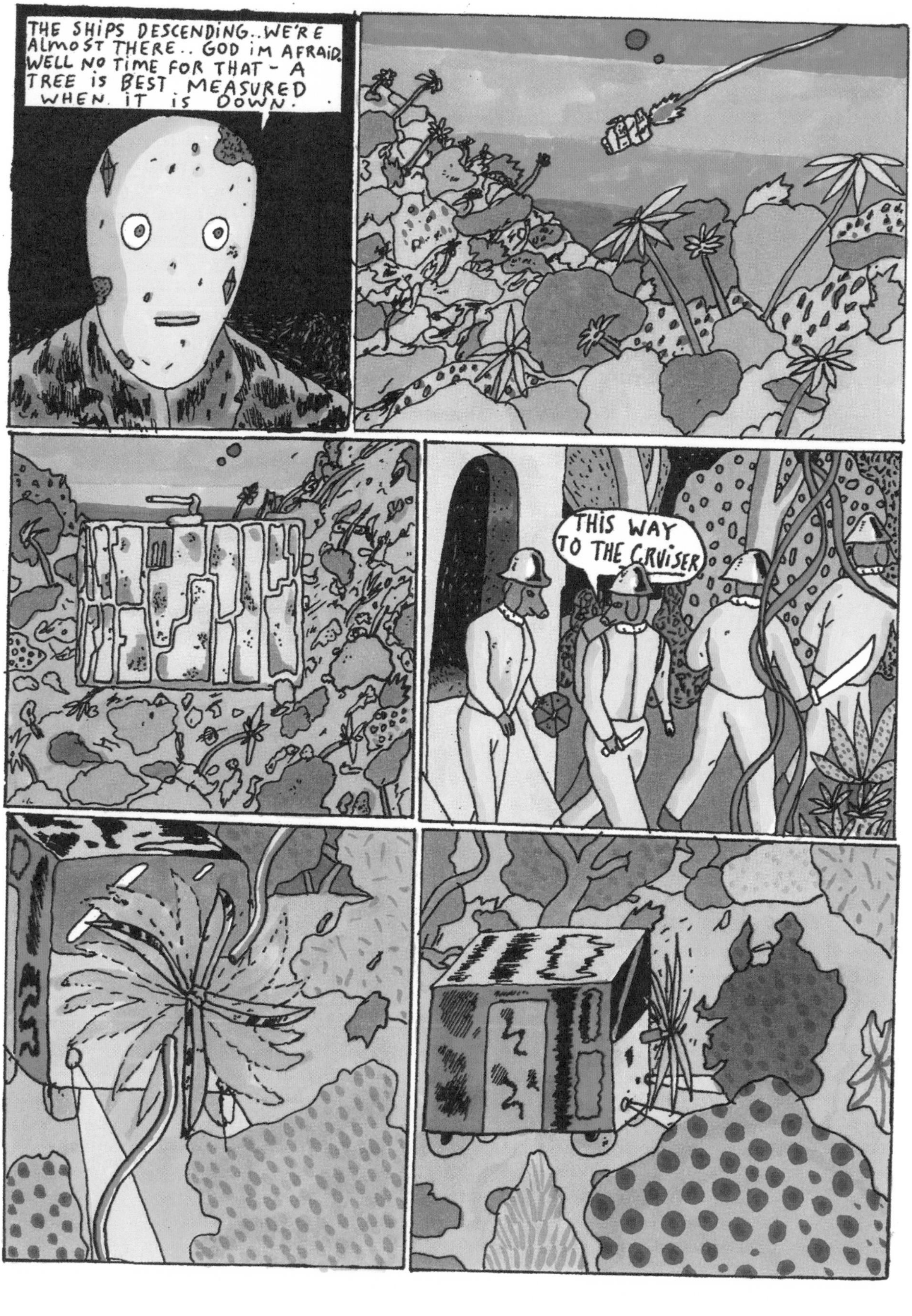
THE SHIPS DESCENDING.. WE'RE ALMOST THERE.. GOD IM AFRAID. WELL NO TIME FOR THAT - A TREE IS BEST MEASURED WHEN IT IS DOWN.
THIS WAY TO THE CRUISER

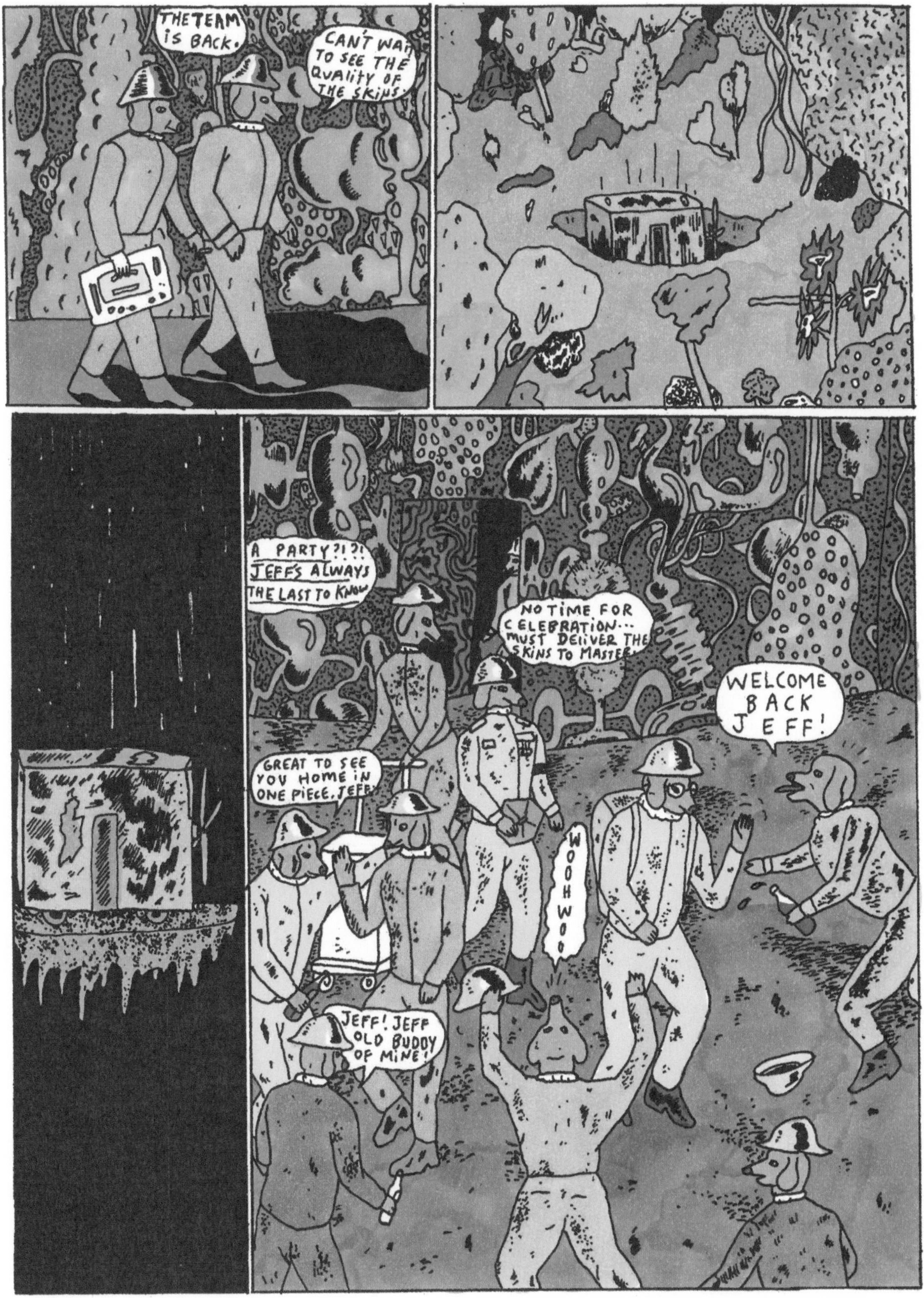
THE TEAM IS BACK.
CAN'T WAIT TO SEE THE QUALITY OF THE SKINS.
A PARTY?!?! JEFF'S ALWAYS THE LAST TO KNOW
NO TIME FOR CELEBRATION... MUST DELIVER THE SKINS TO MASTER.
WELCOME BACK JEFF!
GREAT TO SEE YOU HOME IN ONE PIECE, JEFF.
WOOHWOO
JEFF! JEFF OLD BUDDY OF MINE!

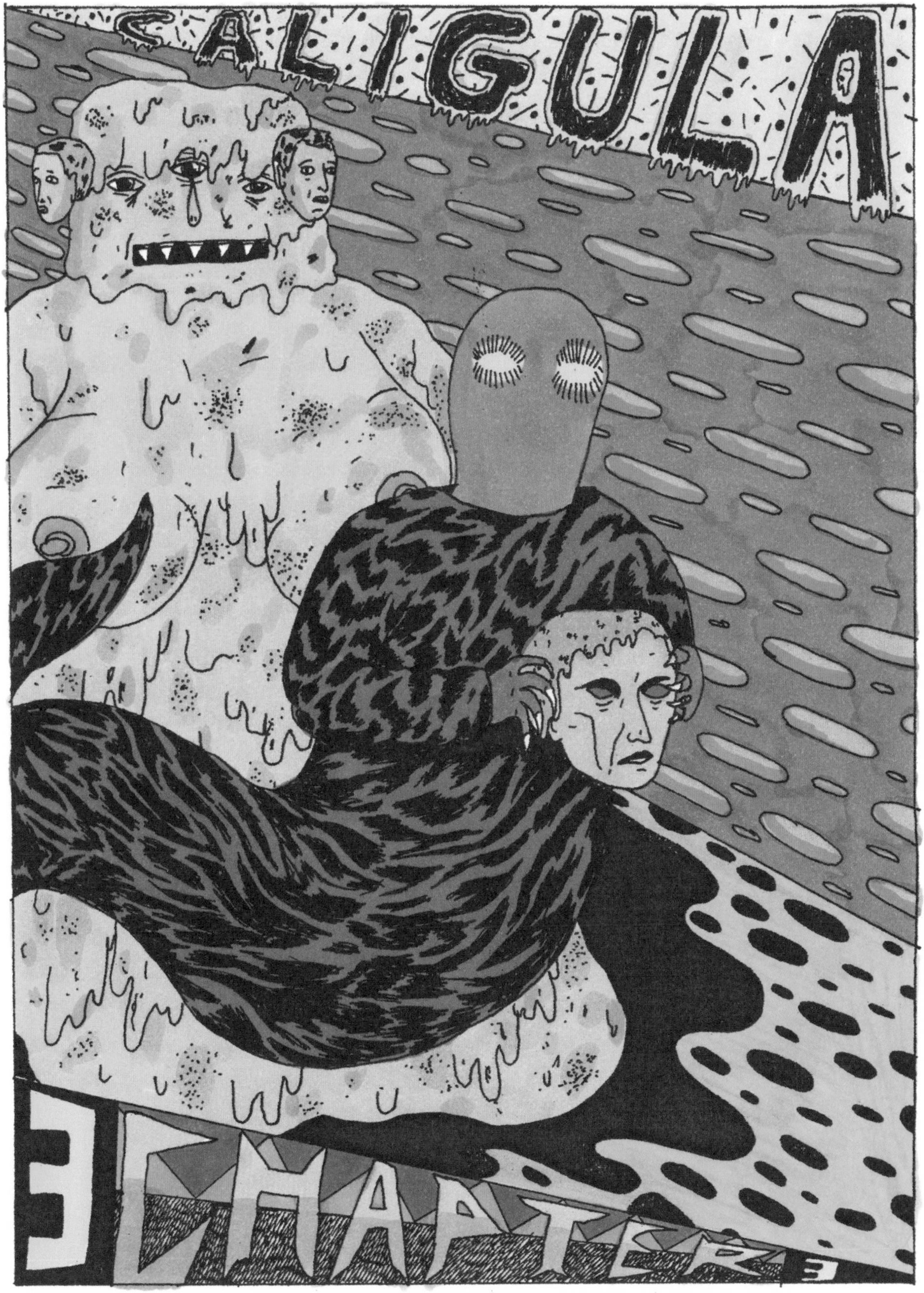
CALIGULA
CHAPTER 3

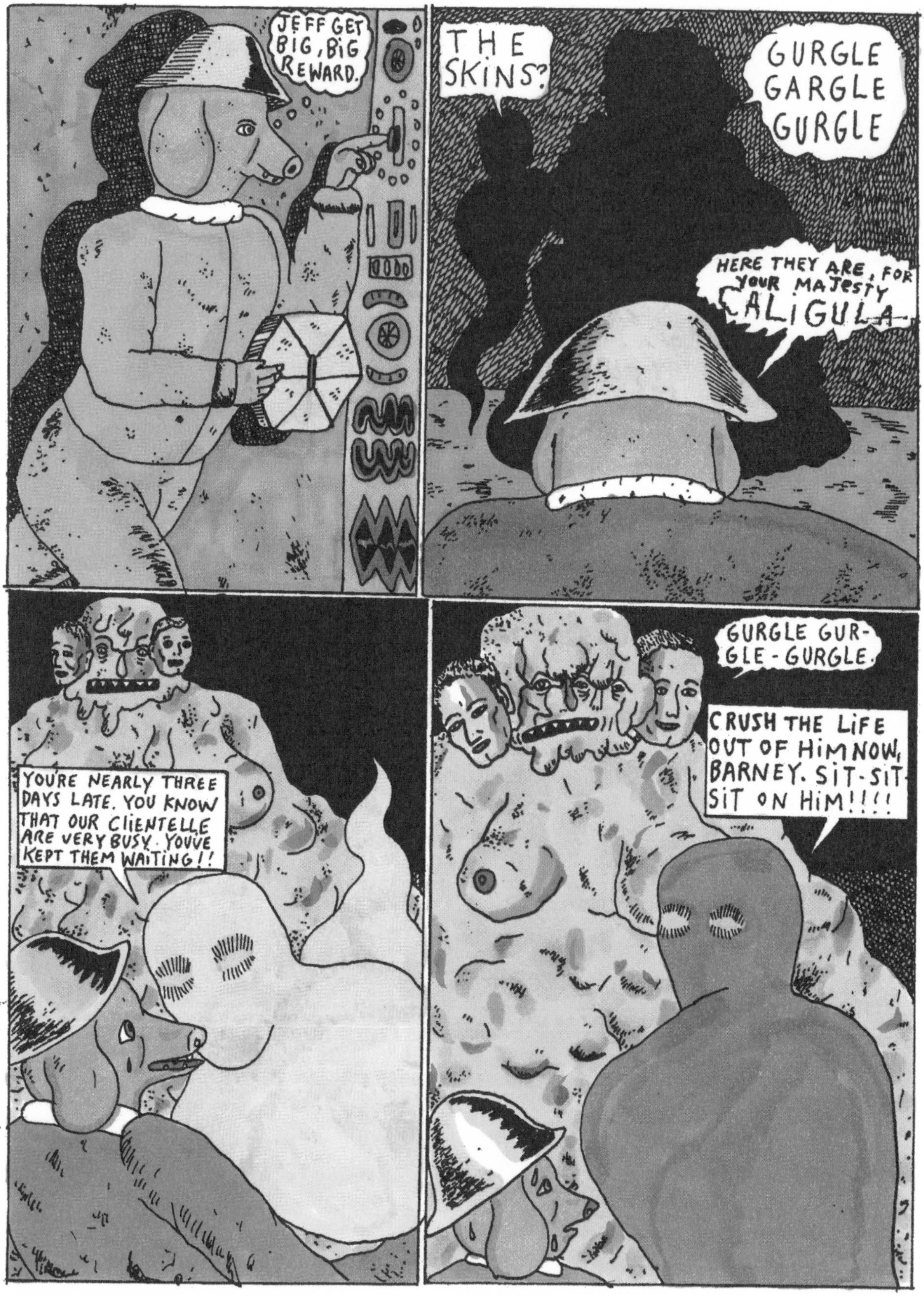
JEFF GET BIG, BIG REWARD.
THE SKINS?
GURGLE GARGLE GURGLE
HERE THEY ARE, FOR YOUR MAJESTY CALIGULA
YOU'RE NEARLY THREE DAYS LATE. YOU KNOW THAT OUR CLIENTELLE ARE VERY BUSY. YOU'VE KEPT THEM WAITING!!
GURGLE GUR-GLE-GURGLE.
CRUSH THE LIFE OUT OF HIM NOW, BARNEY. SIT-SIT-SIT ON HIM!!!!

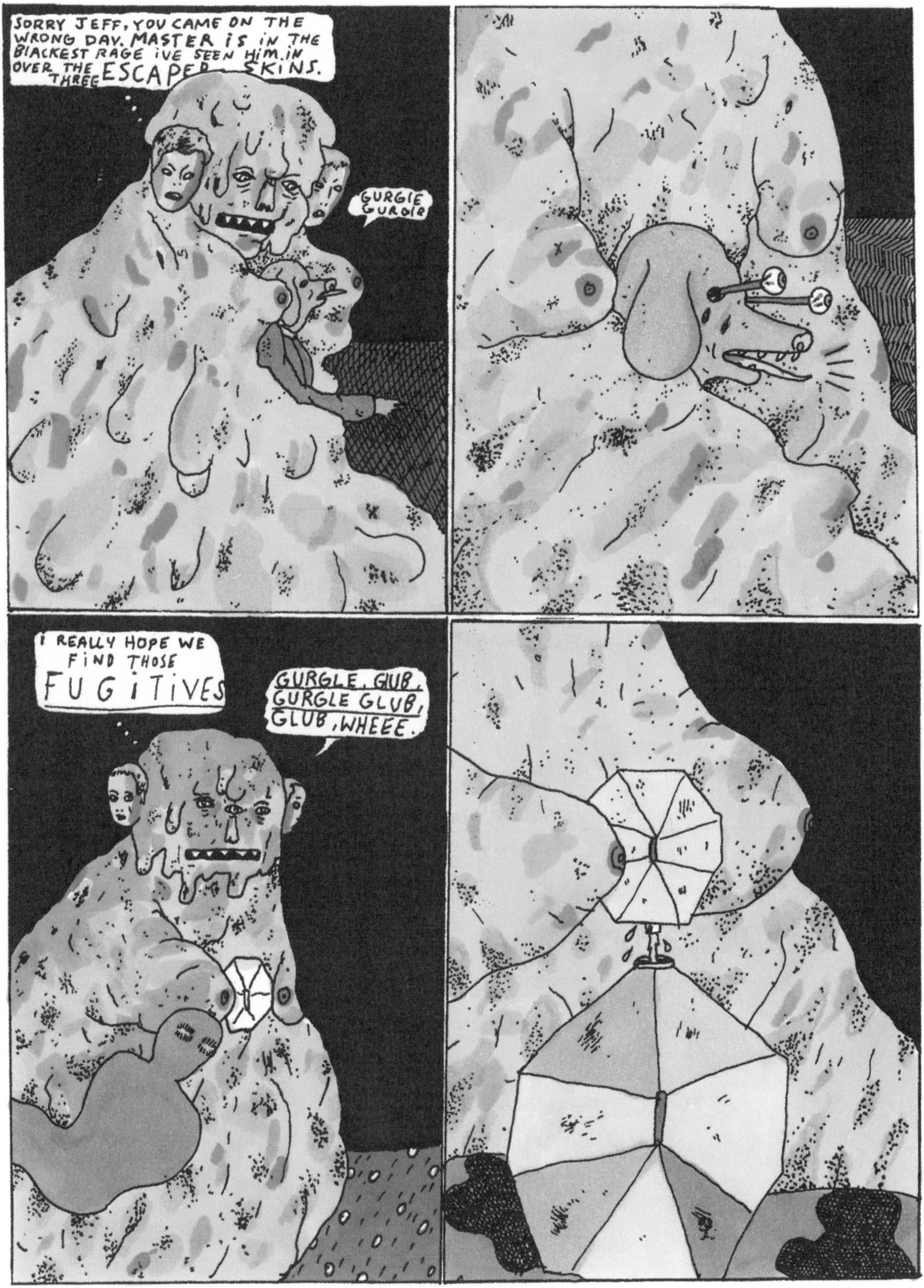
SORRY JEFF, YOU CAME ON THE WRONG DAY. MASTER IS IN THE BLACKEST RAGE IVE SEEN HIM IN OVER THE THREE ESCAPED SKINS.
GURGLE GURGLE
I REALLY HOPE WE FIND THOSE FUGITIVES
GURGLE. GLUB, GURGLE GLUB, GLUB, WHEEE.

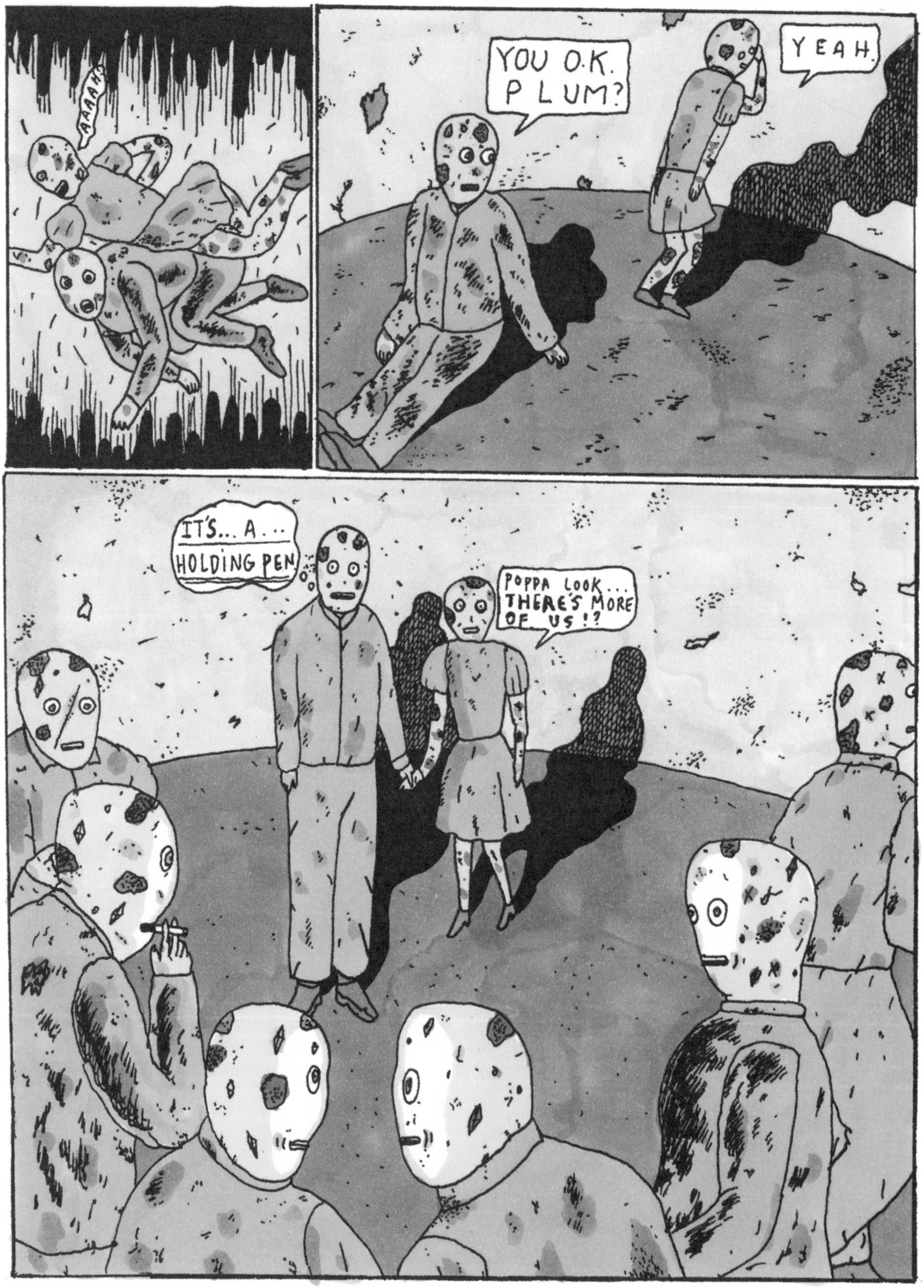
AAAAH
YOU O.K. PLUM?
YEAH.
IT'S... A... HOLDING PEN
POPPA LOOK... THERE'S MORE OF US!?

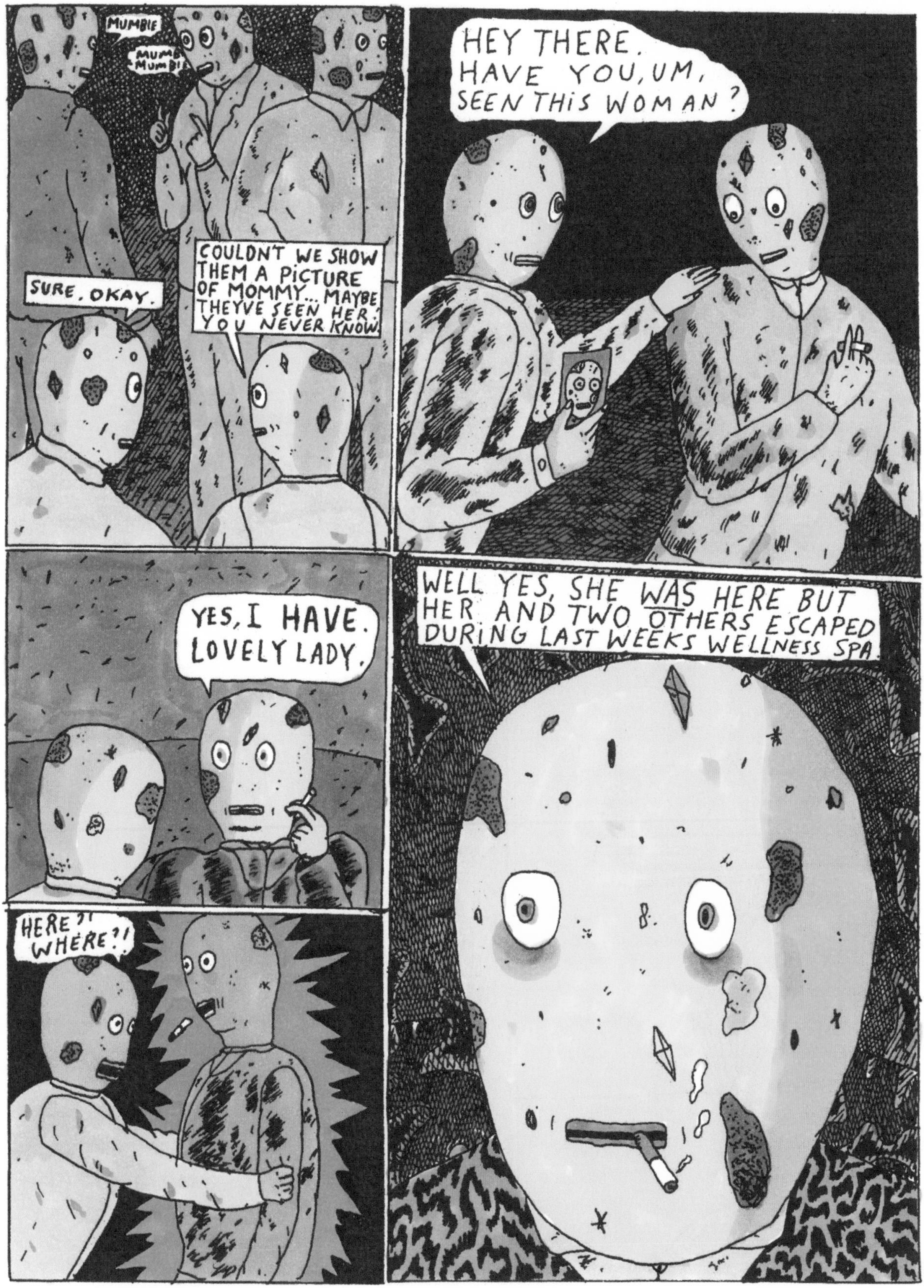
MUMBIE
MUMBIE MUMBIE
SURE, OKAY.
COULDN'T WE SHOW THEM A PICTURE OF MOMMY... MAYBE THEY'VE SEEN HER. YOU NEVER KNOW.
HEY THERE. HAVE YOU, UM, SEEN THIS WOMAN?
YES, I HAVE. LOVELY LADY.
WELL YES, SHE WAS HERE BUT HER AND TWO OTHERS ESCAPED DURING LAST WEEKS WELLNESS SPA.
HERE?! WHERE?!

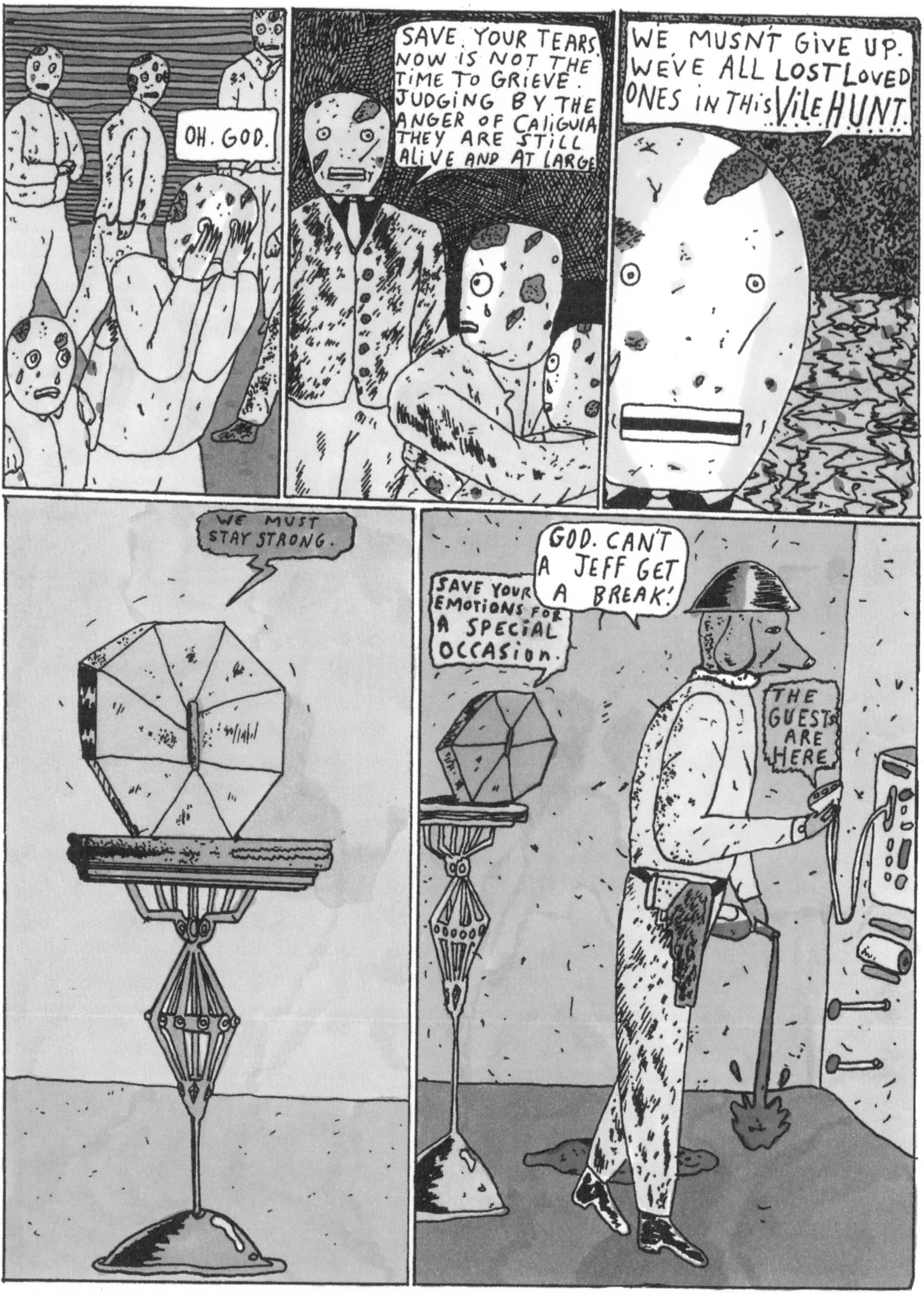
OH. GOD.
SAVE YOUR TEARS NOW IS NOT THE TIME TO GRIEVE. JUDGING BY THE ANGER OF CALIGULA THEY ARE STILL ALIVE AND AT LARGE
WE MUSN'T GIVE UP. WE'VE ALL LOST LOVED ONES IN THIS VILE HUNT.
WE MUST STAY STRONG.
SAVE YOUR EMOTIONS FOR A SPECIAL OCCASION.
GOD. CAN'T A JEFF GET A BREAK!
THE GUESTS ARE HERE

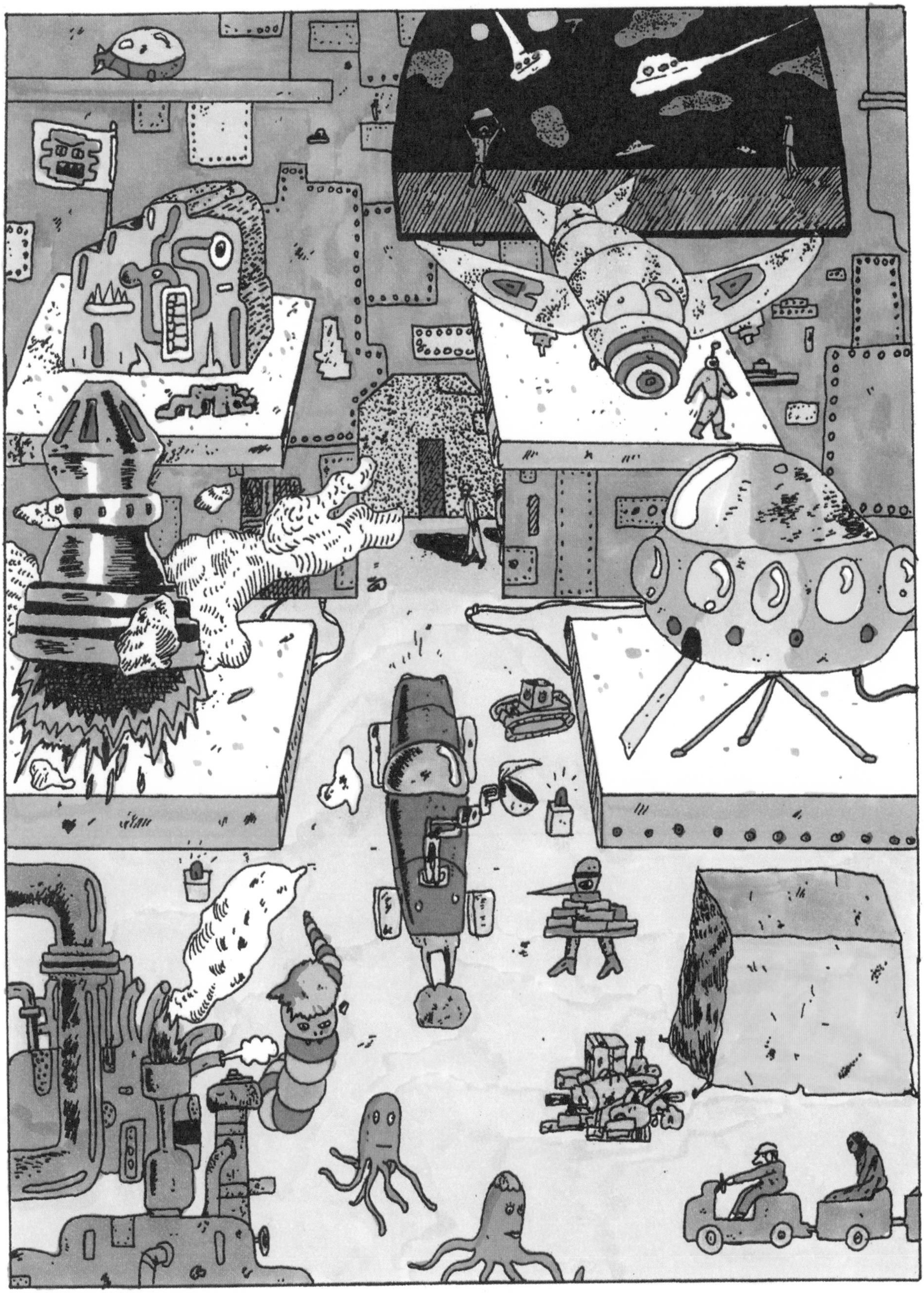

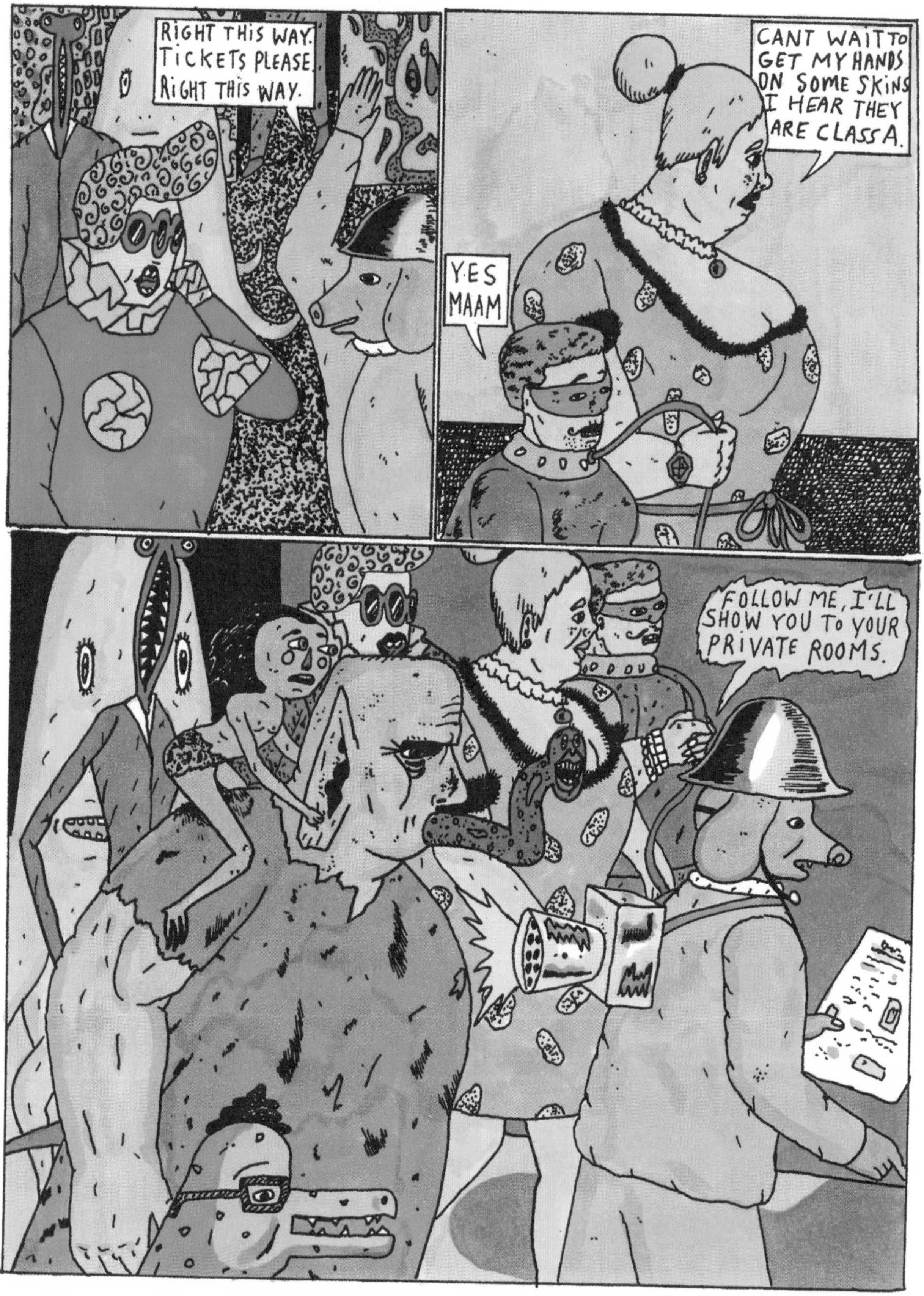
RIGHT THIS WAY. TICKETS PLEASE. RIGHT THIS WAY.
CANT WAIT TO GET MY HANDS ON SOME SKINS I HEAR THEY ARE CLASS A.
YES MAAM
FOLLOW ME, I'LL SHOW YOU TO YOUR PRIVATE ROOMS.

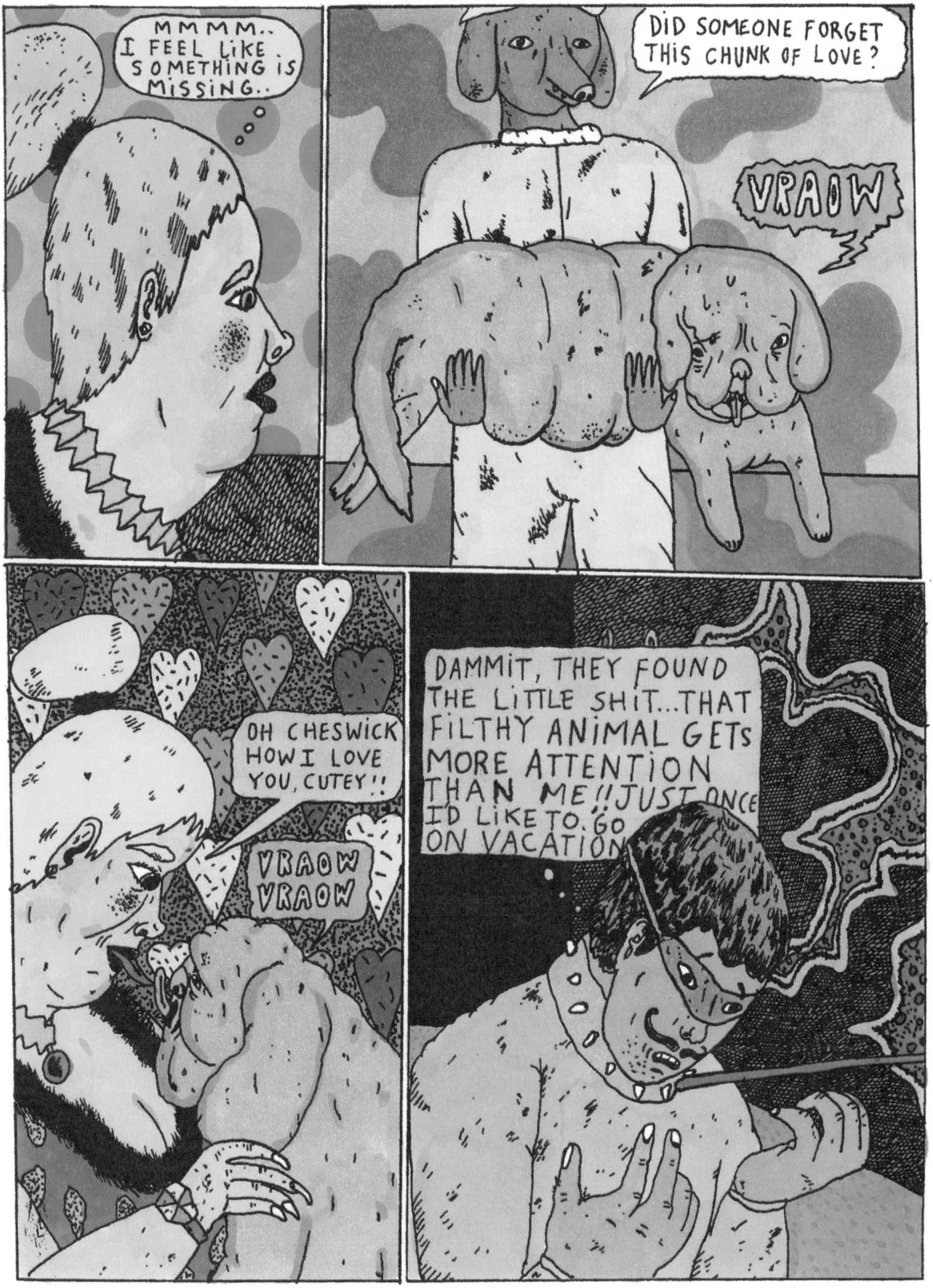
MMMMM..
I FEEL LIKE SOMETHING IS MISSING..
DID SOMEONE FORGET THIS CHUNK OF LOVE?
VRAOW
OH CHESWICK HOW I LOVE YOU, CUTEY!!
VRAOW VRAOW
DAMMIT, THEY FOUND THE LITTLE SHIT...THAT FILTHY ANIMAL GETS MORE ATTENTION THAN ME!! JUST ONCE I'D LIKE TO GO ON VACATION

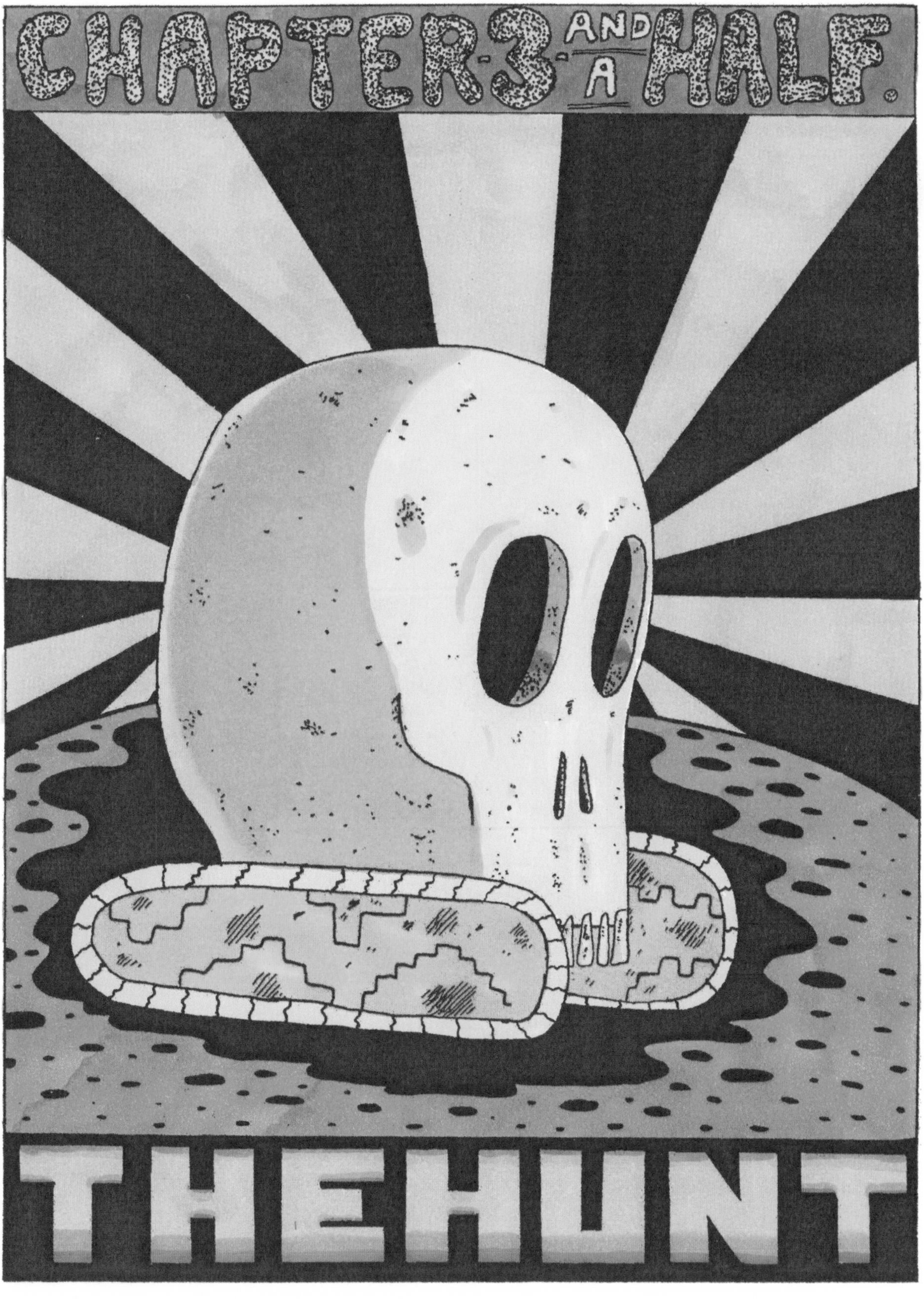
CHAPTER 3 AND A HALF.
THE HUNT

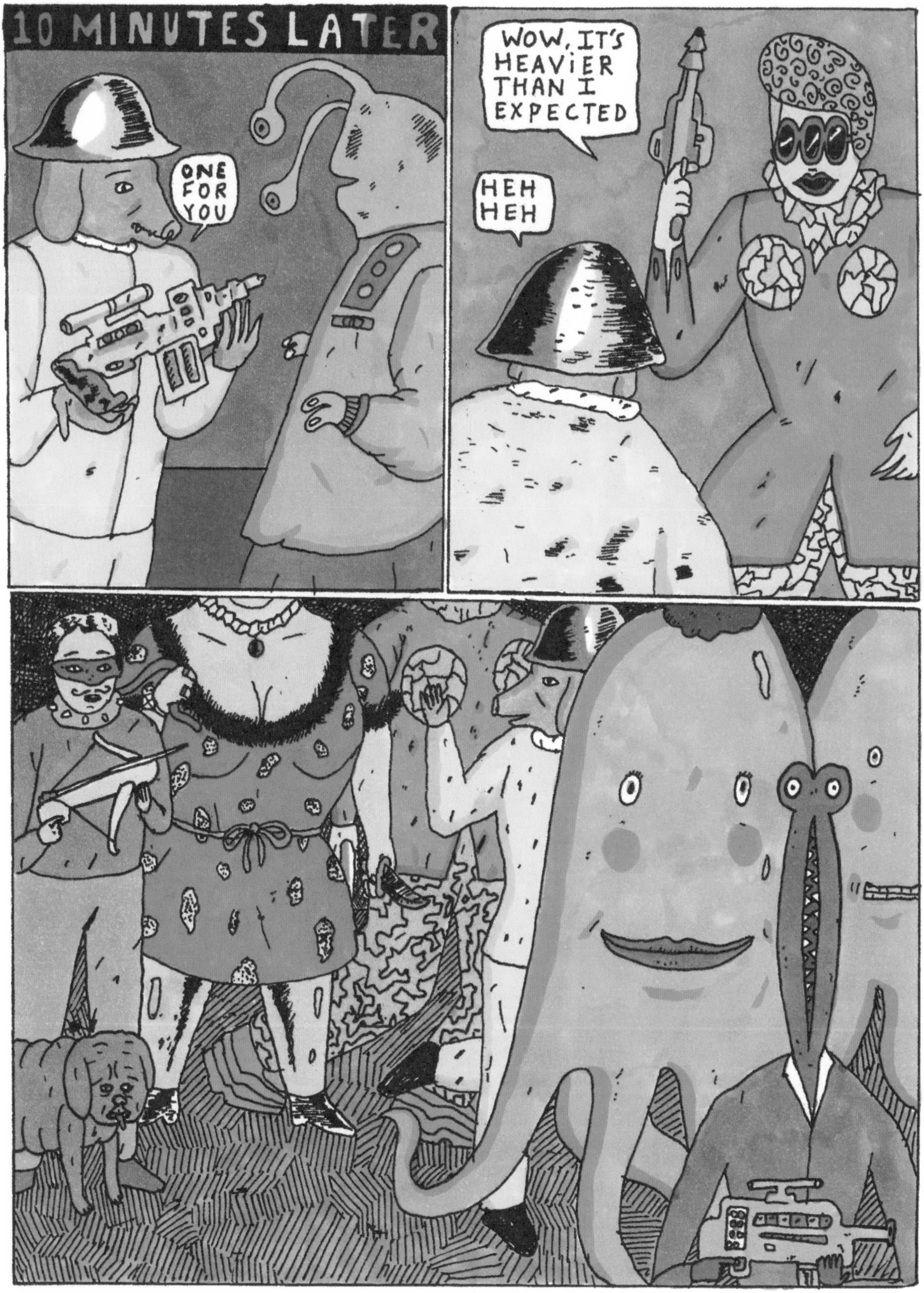
10 MINUTES LATER
ONE FOR YOU
WOW, IT'S HEAVIER THAN I EXPECTED
HEH HEH

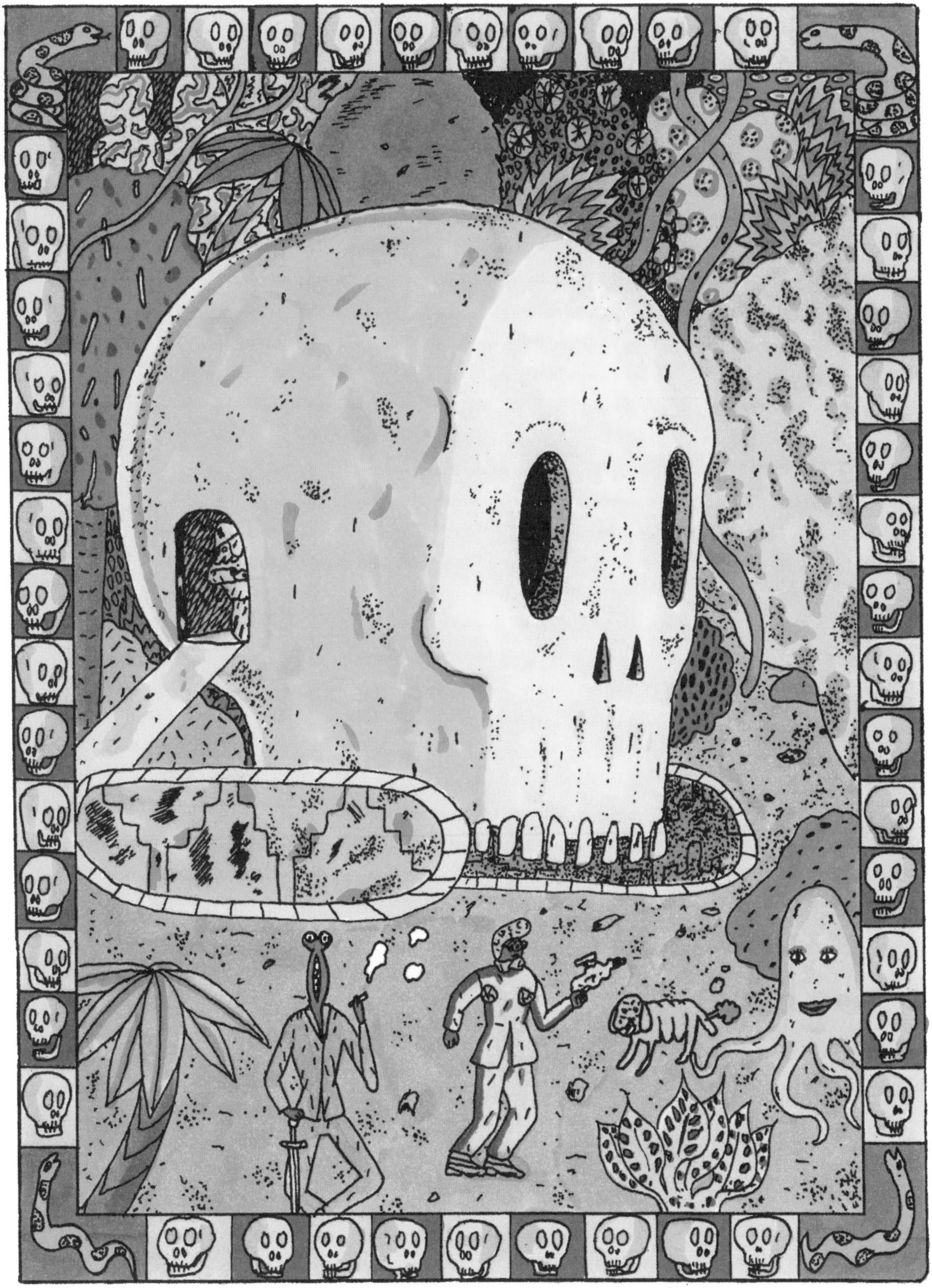

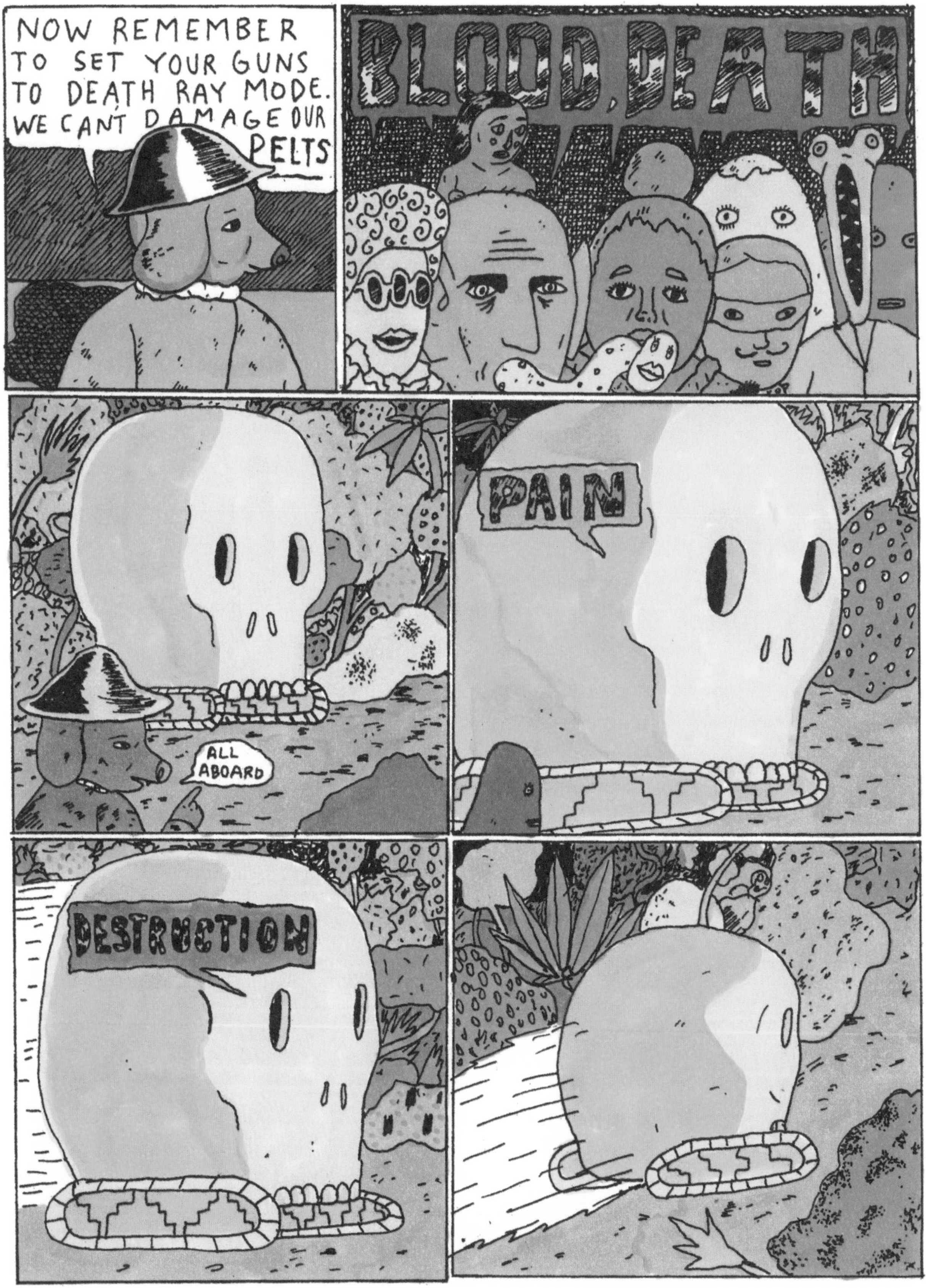
NOW REMEMBER TO SET YOUR GUNS TO DEATH RAY MODE. WE CAN'T DAMAGE OUR PELTS
BLOOD, DEATH
ALL ABOARD
PAIN
DESTRUCTION

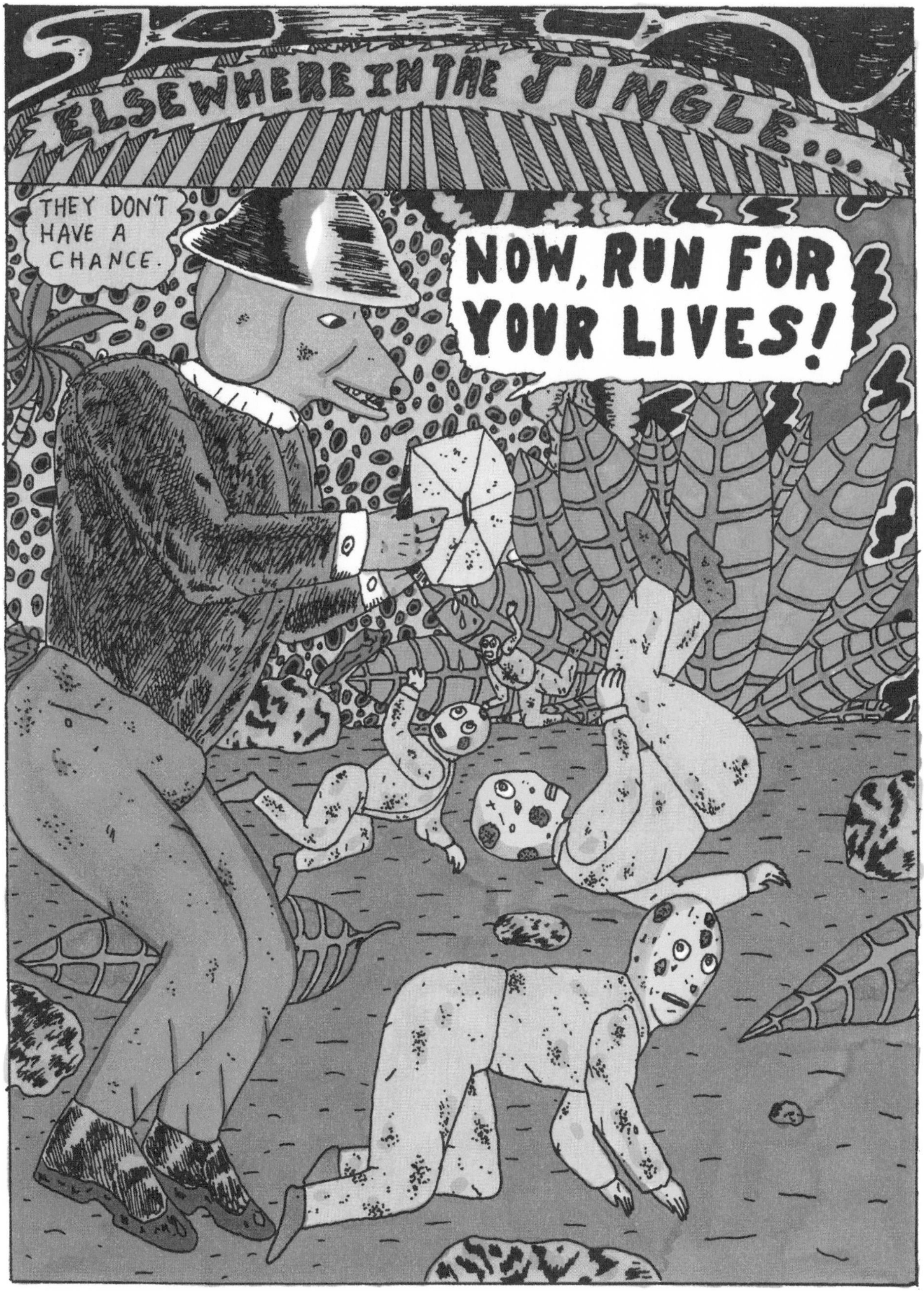
ELSEWHERE IN THE JUNGLE...
THEY DON'T HAVE A CHANCE.
NOW, RUN FOR YOUR LIVES!

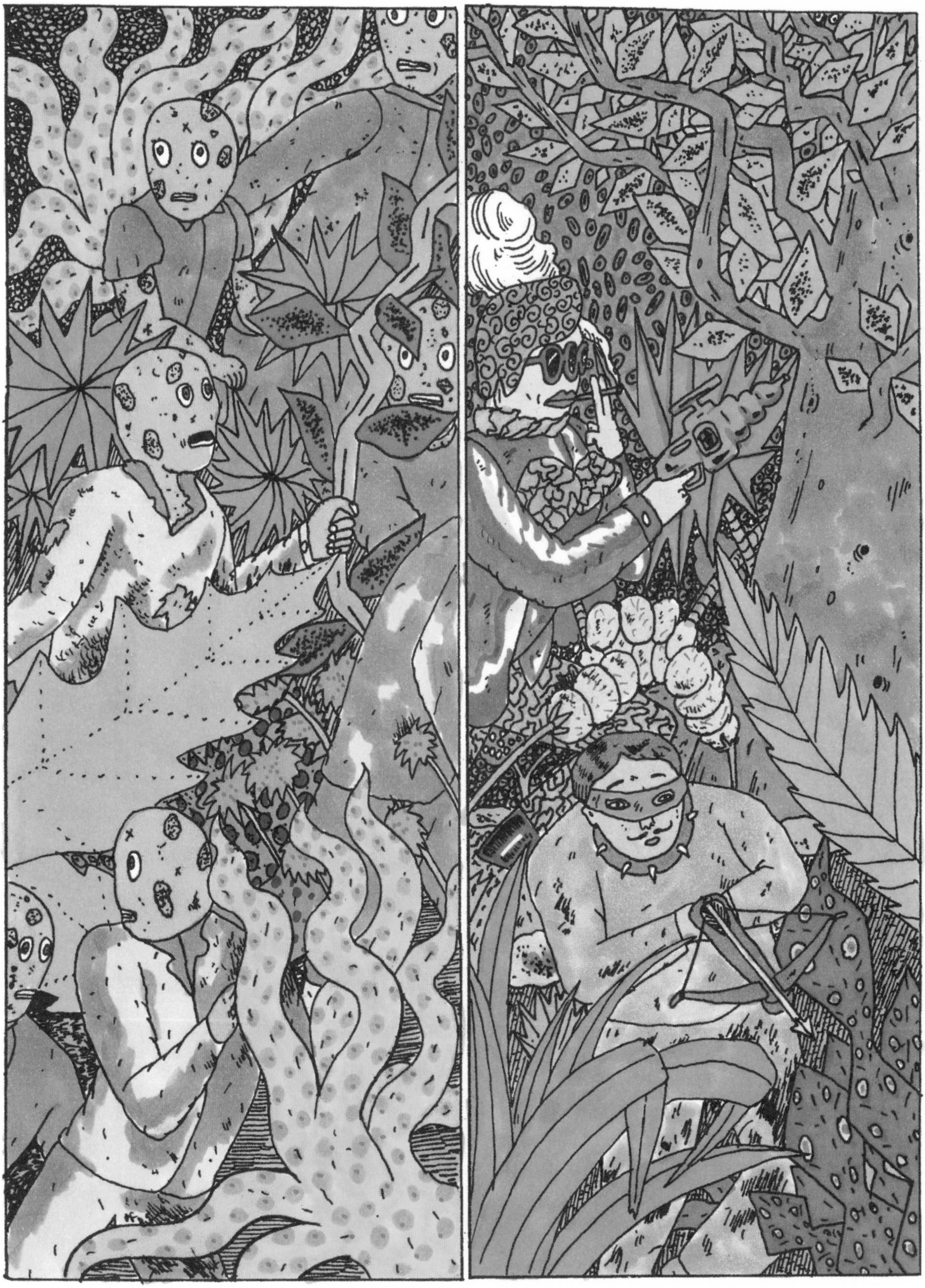

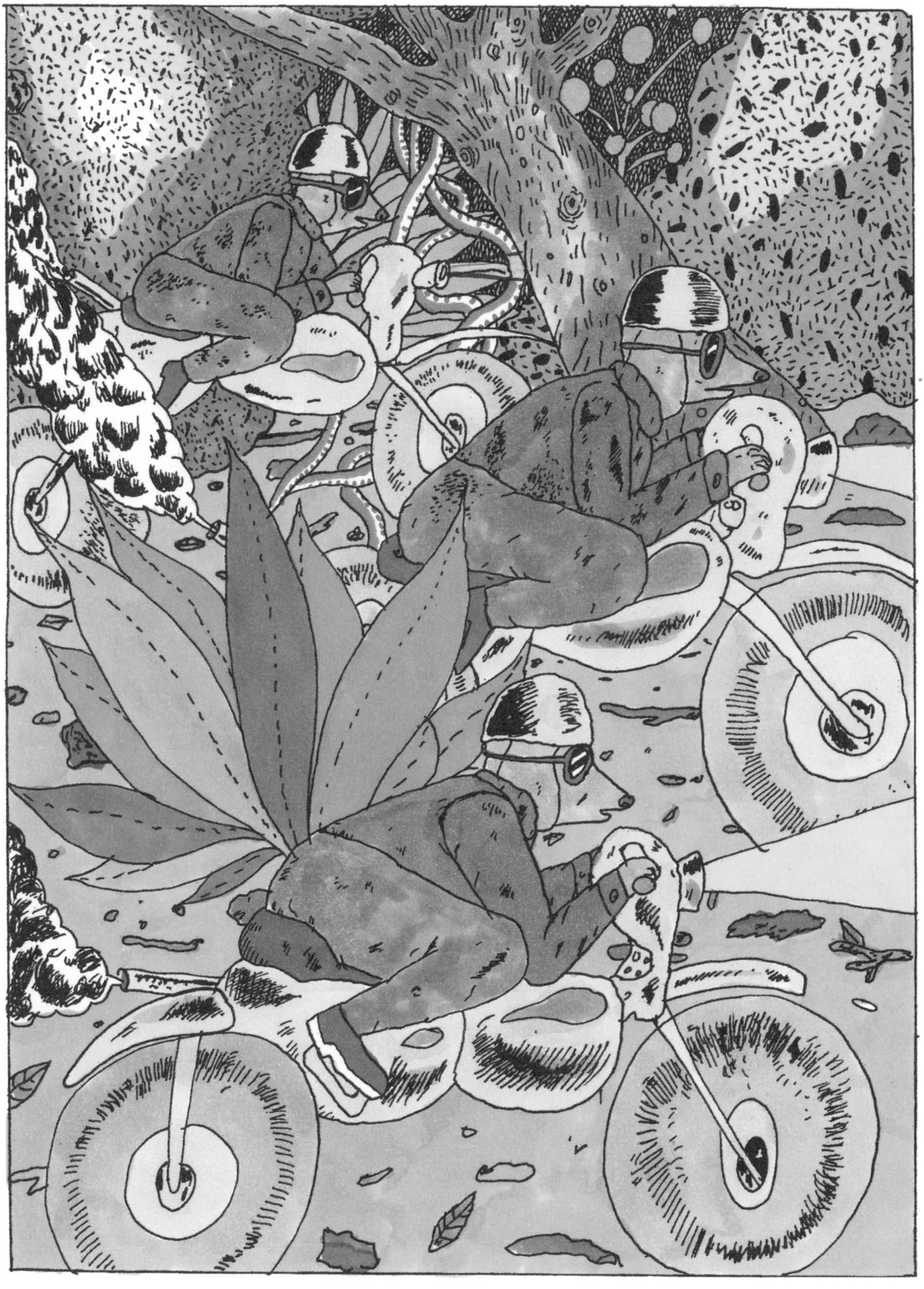

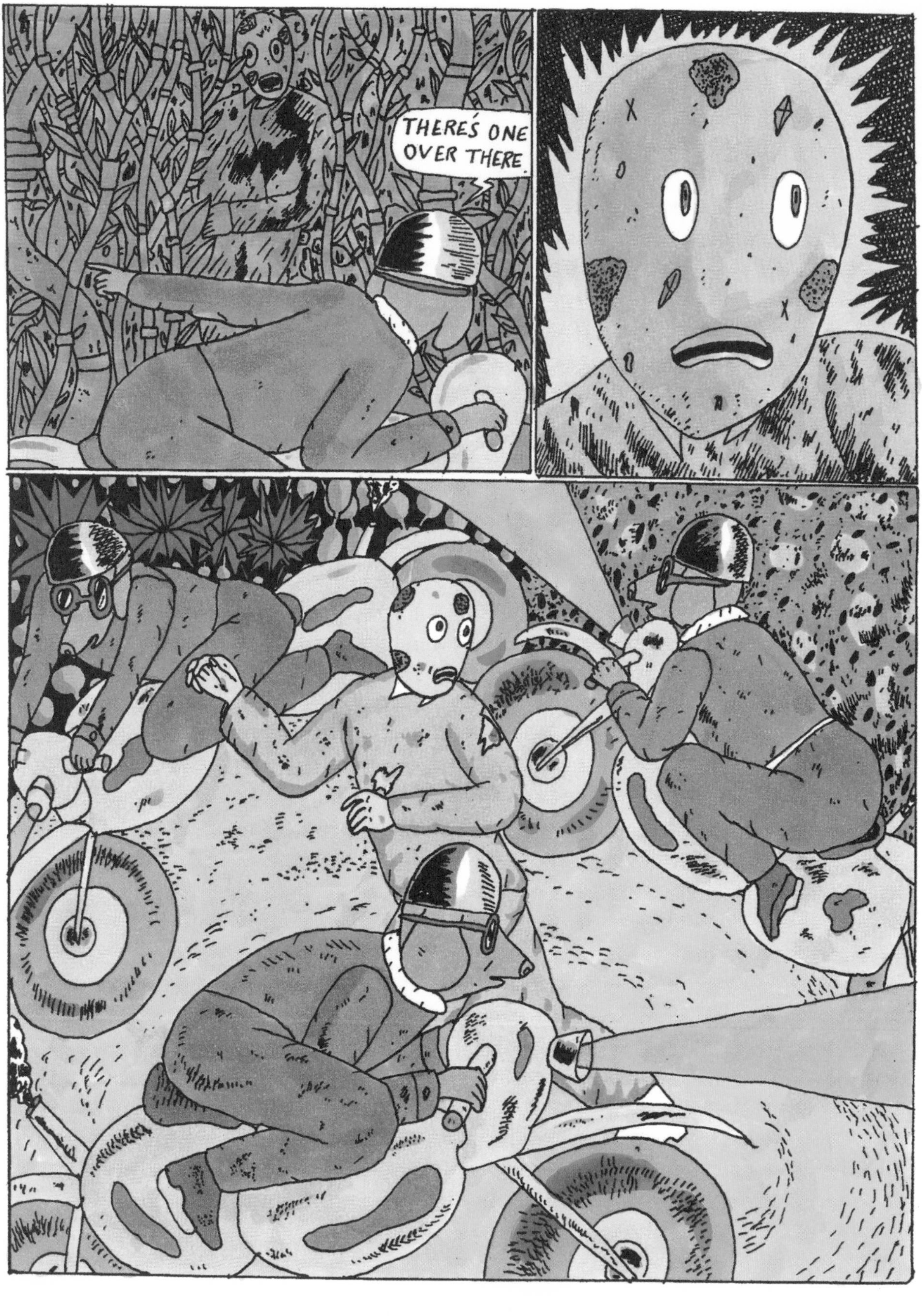
THERE'S ONE OVER THERE

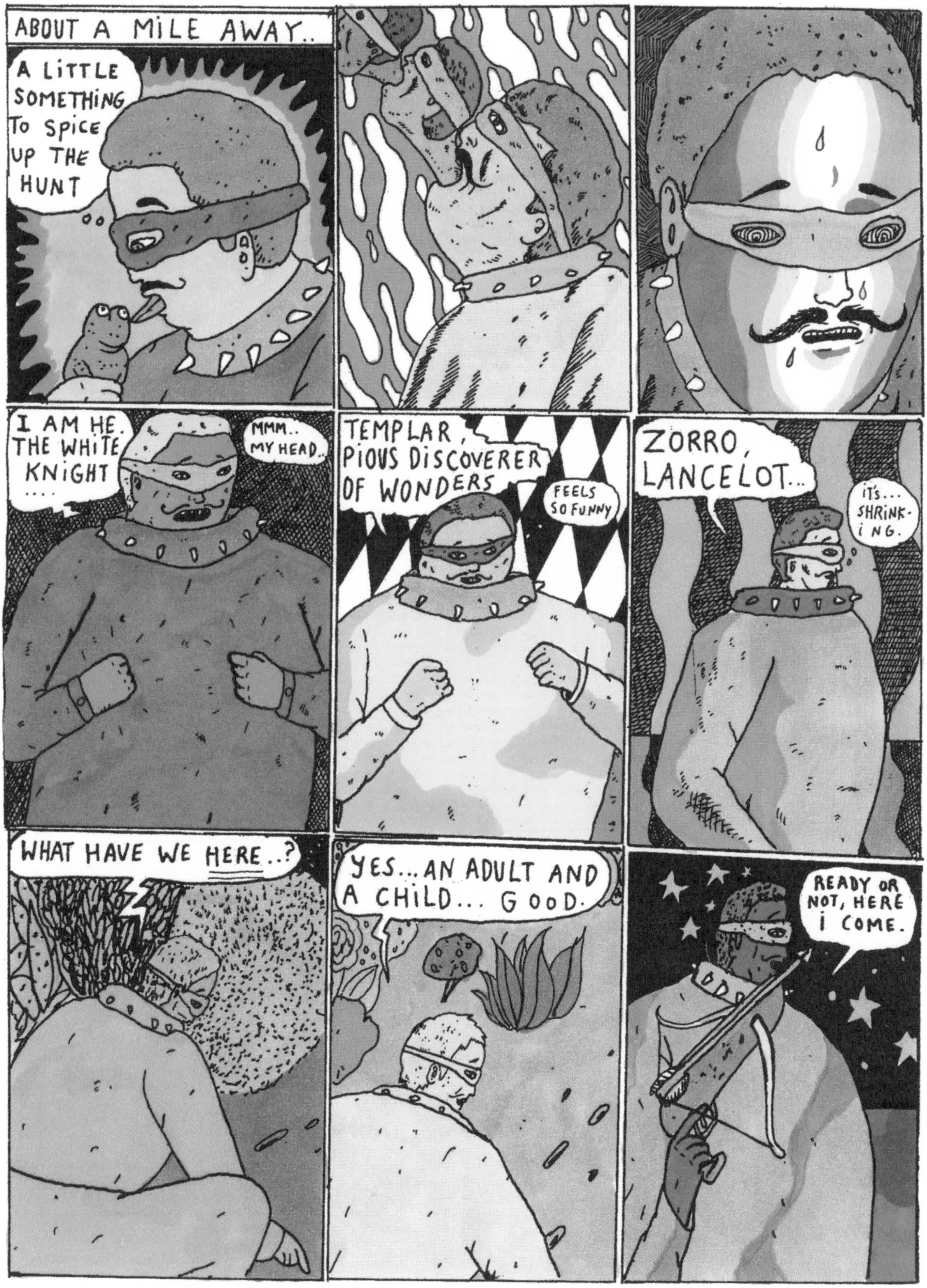
ABOUT A MILE AWAY..
A LITTLE SOMETHING TO SPICE UP THE HUNT
I AM HE. THE WHITE KNIGHT ....
MMM.. MY HEAD..
TEMPLAR, PIOUS DISCOVERER OF WONDERS
FEELS SO FUNNY
ZORRO, LANCELOT...
IT'S... SHRINK-ING.
WHAT HAVE WE HERE..?
YES... AN ADULT AND A CHILD... GOOD.
READY OR NOT, HERE I COME.

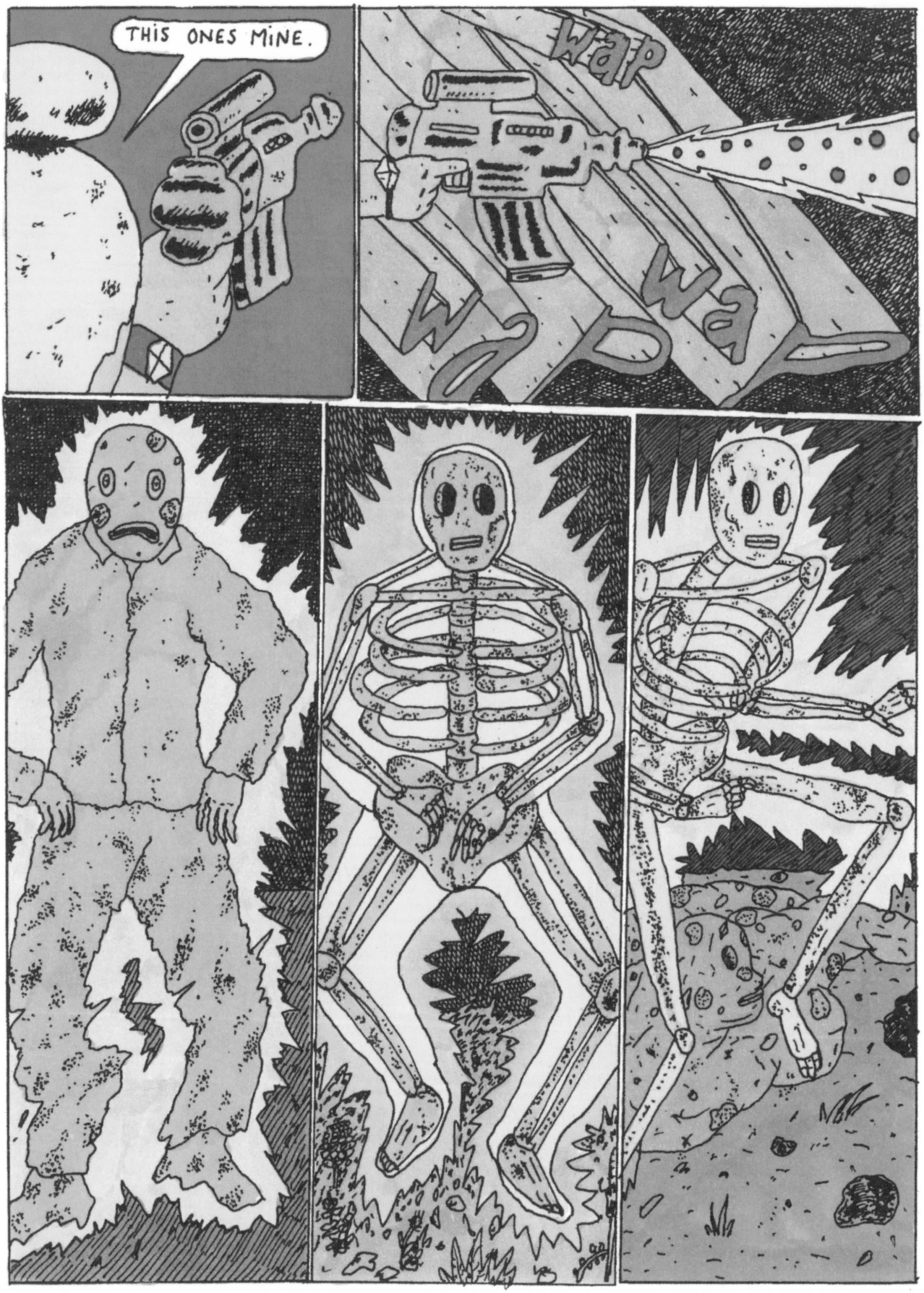
THIS ONES MINE.
WAP
WAP
WAP

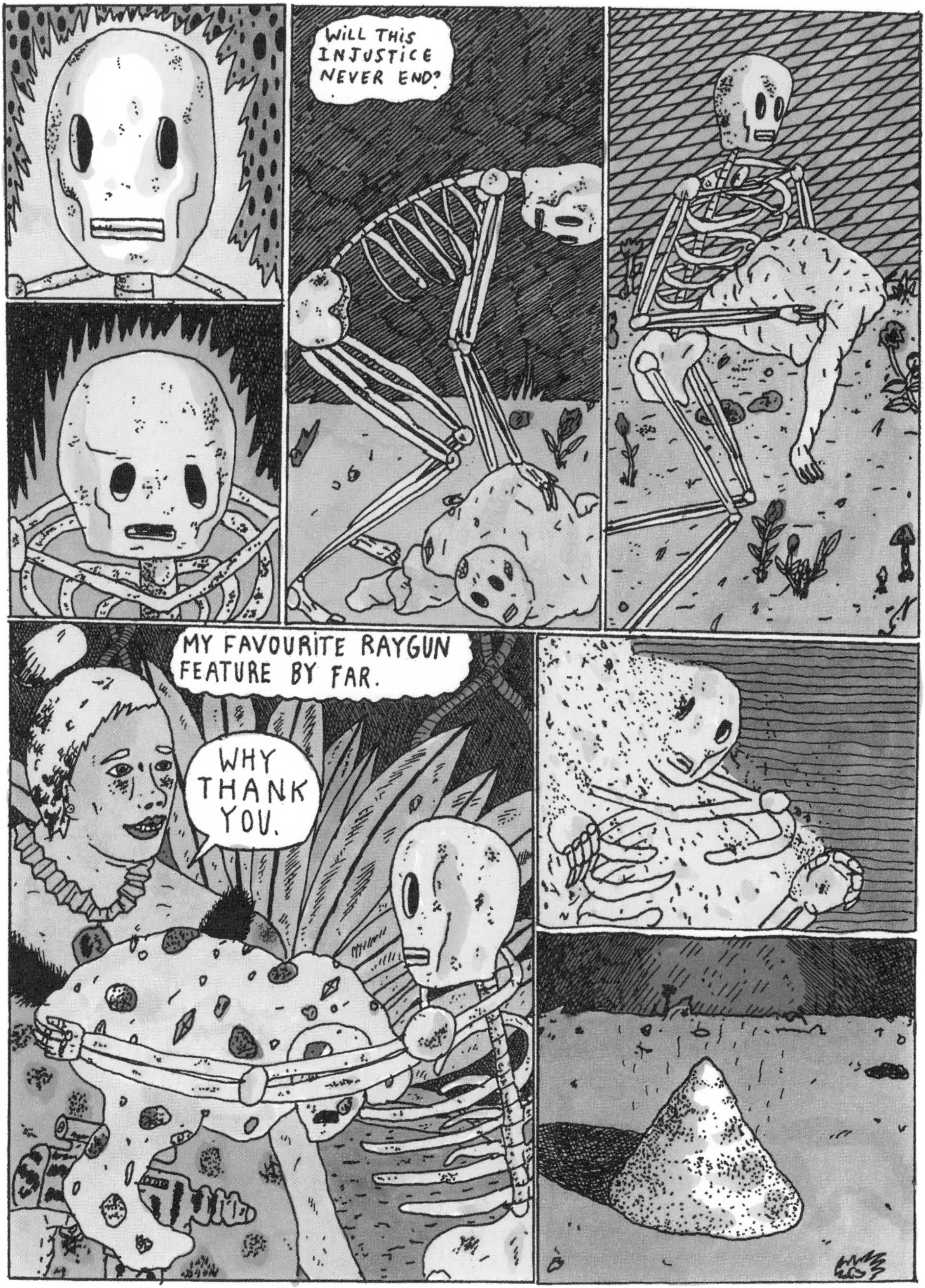
WILL THIS INJUSTICE NEVER END?
MY FAVOURITE RAYGUN FEATURE BY FAR.
WHY THANK YOU.

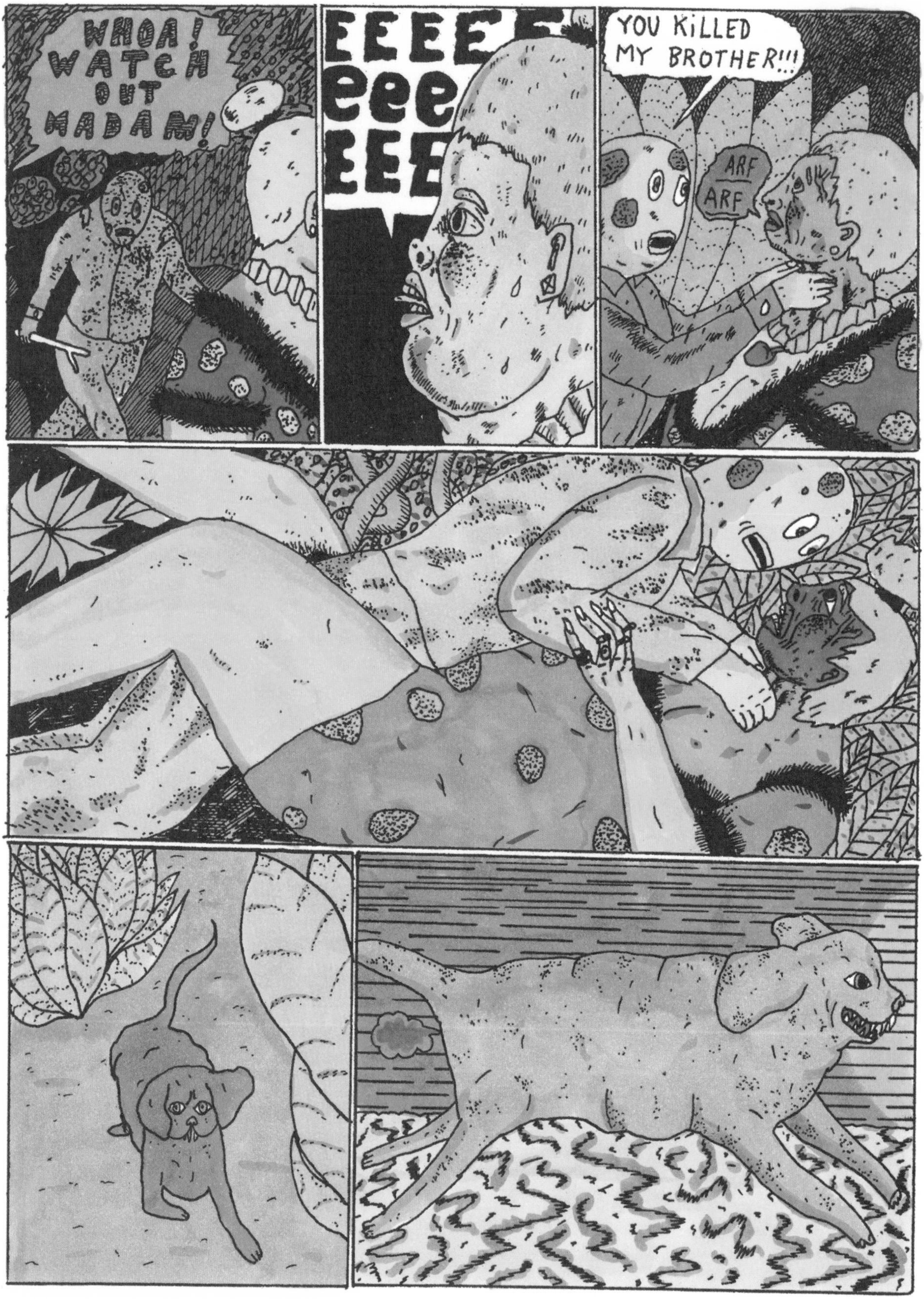
WHOA! WATCH OUT MADAM!
EEEE eee EEE
YOU KILLED MY BROTHER!!!
ARF ARF

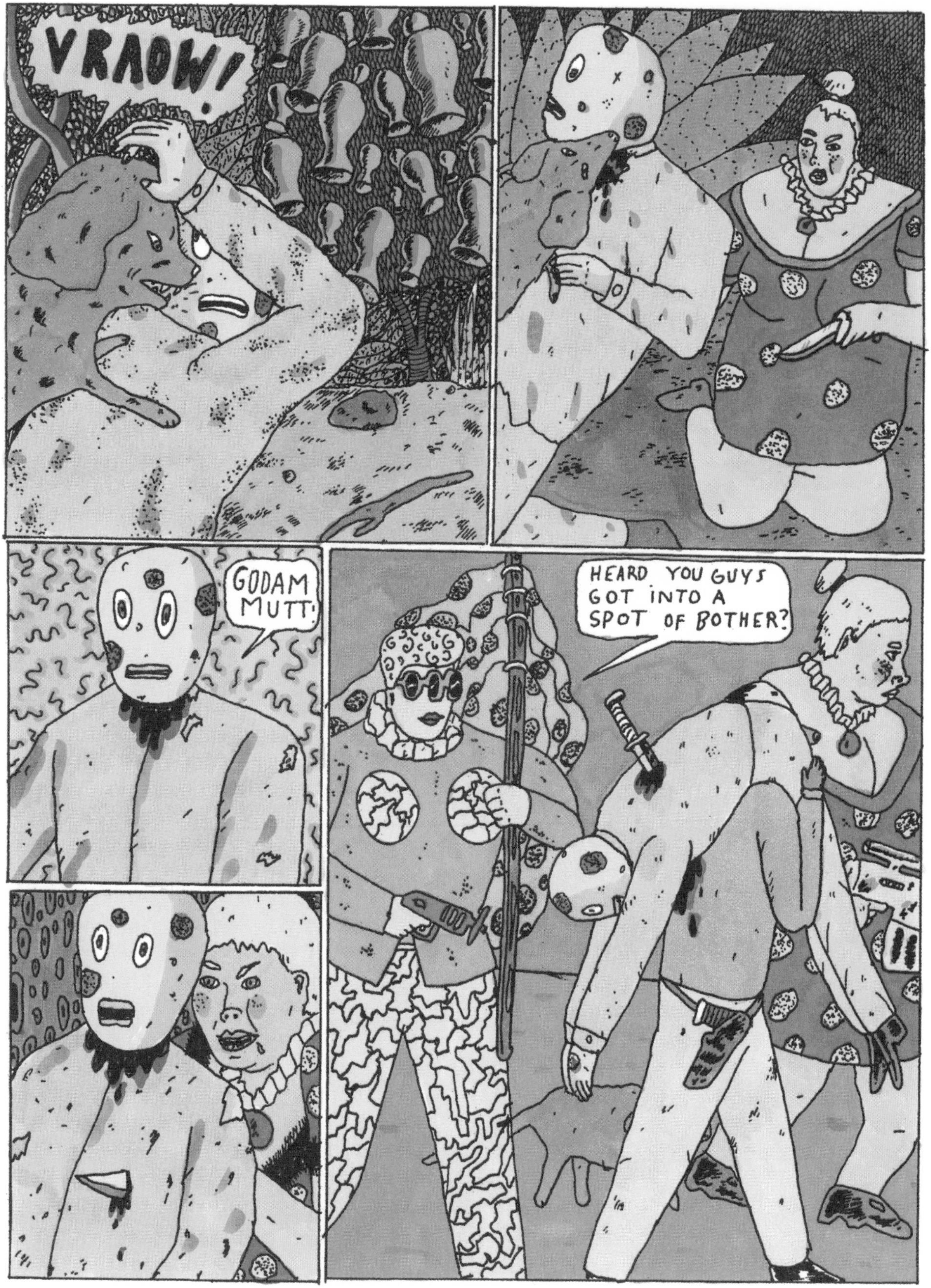
VRAOW!
GODAM MUTT!
HEARD YOU GUYS GOT INTO A SPOT OF BOTHER?

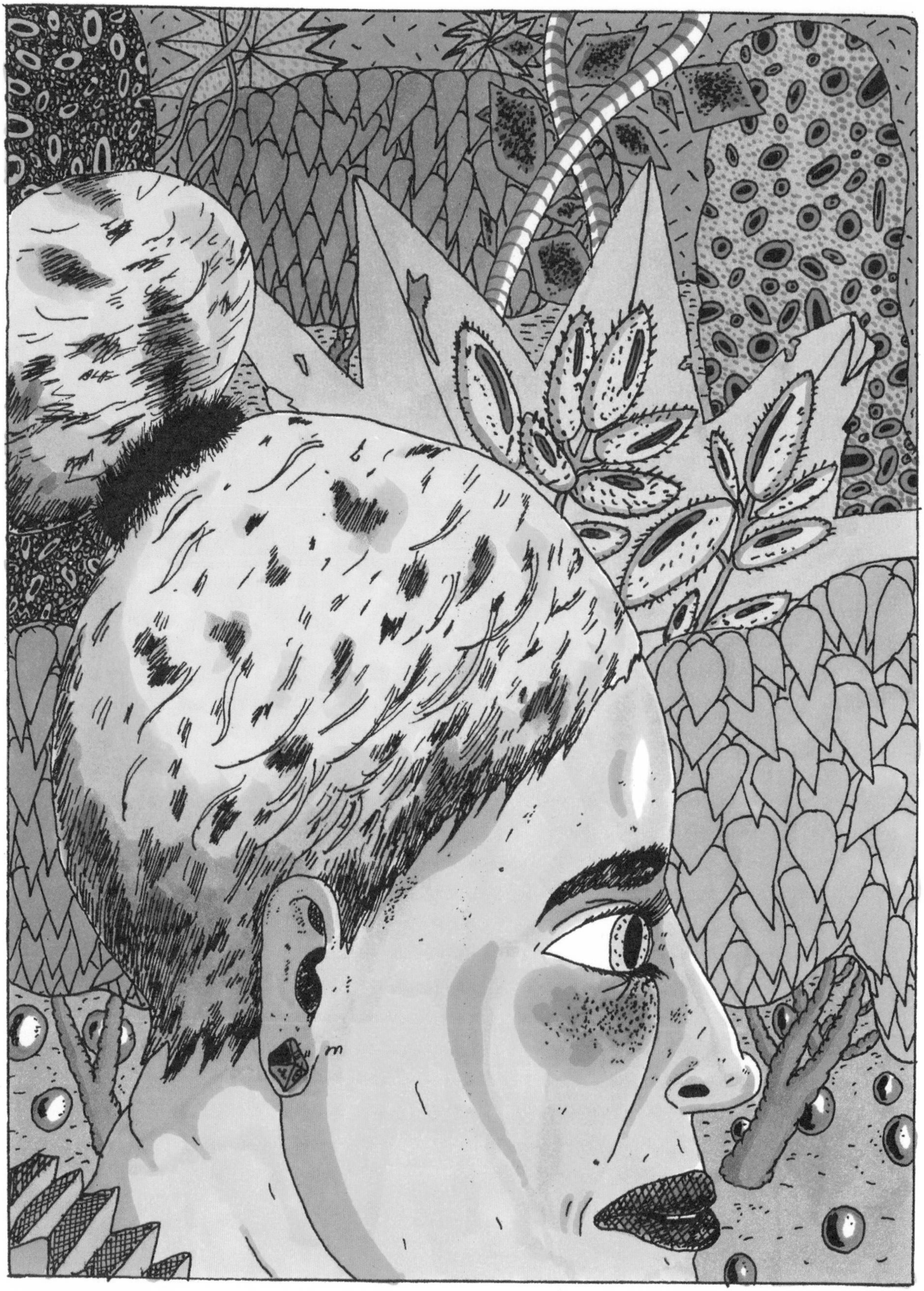

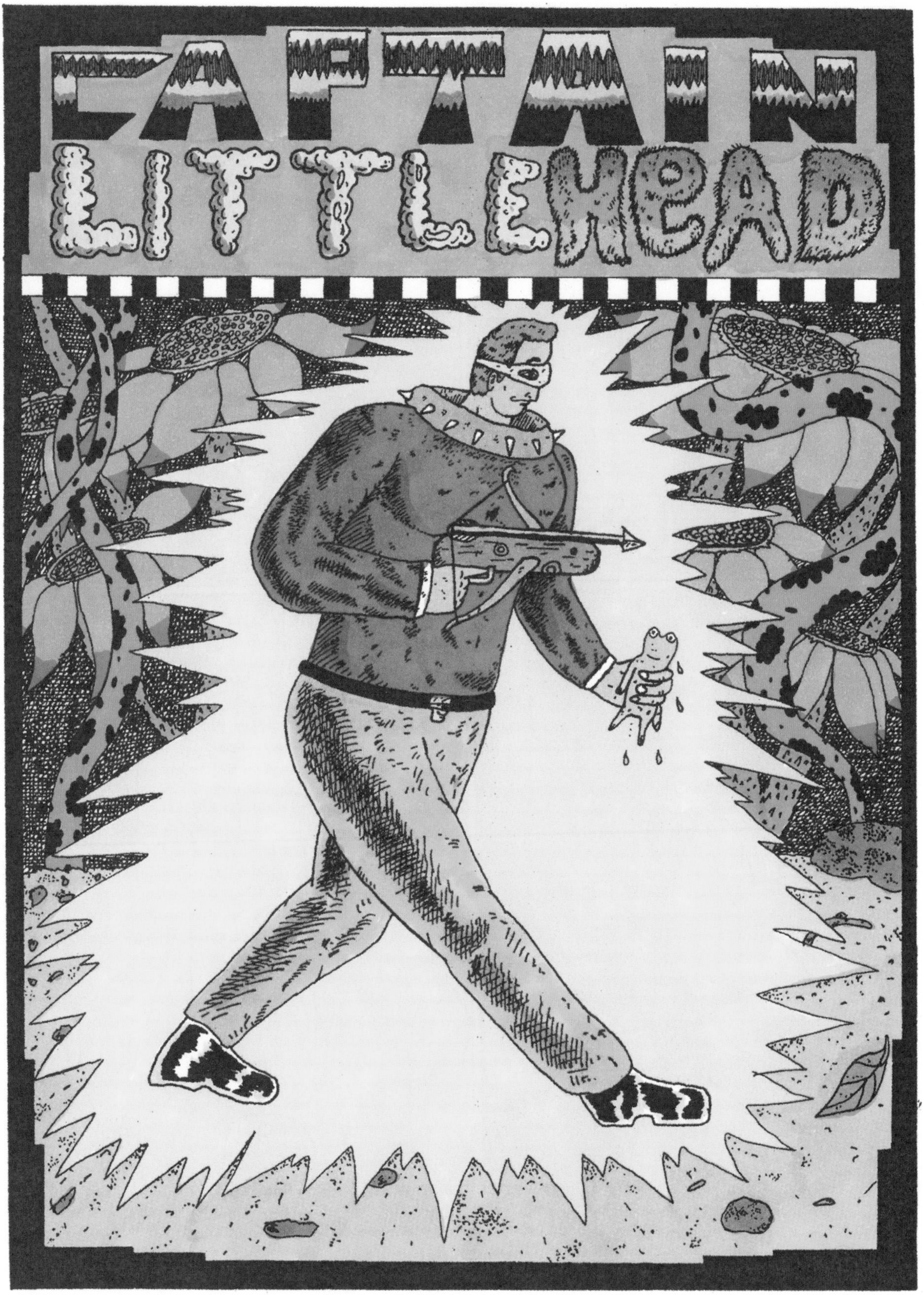
CAPTAIN
LITTLEHEAD

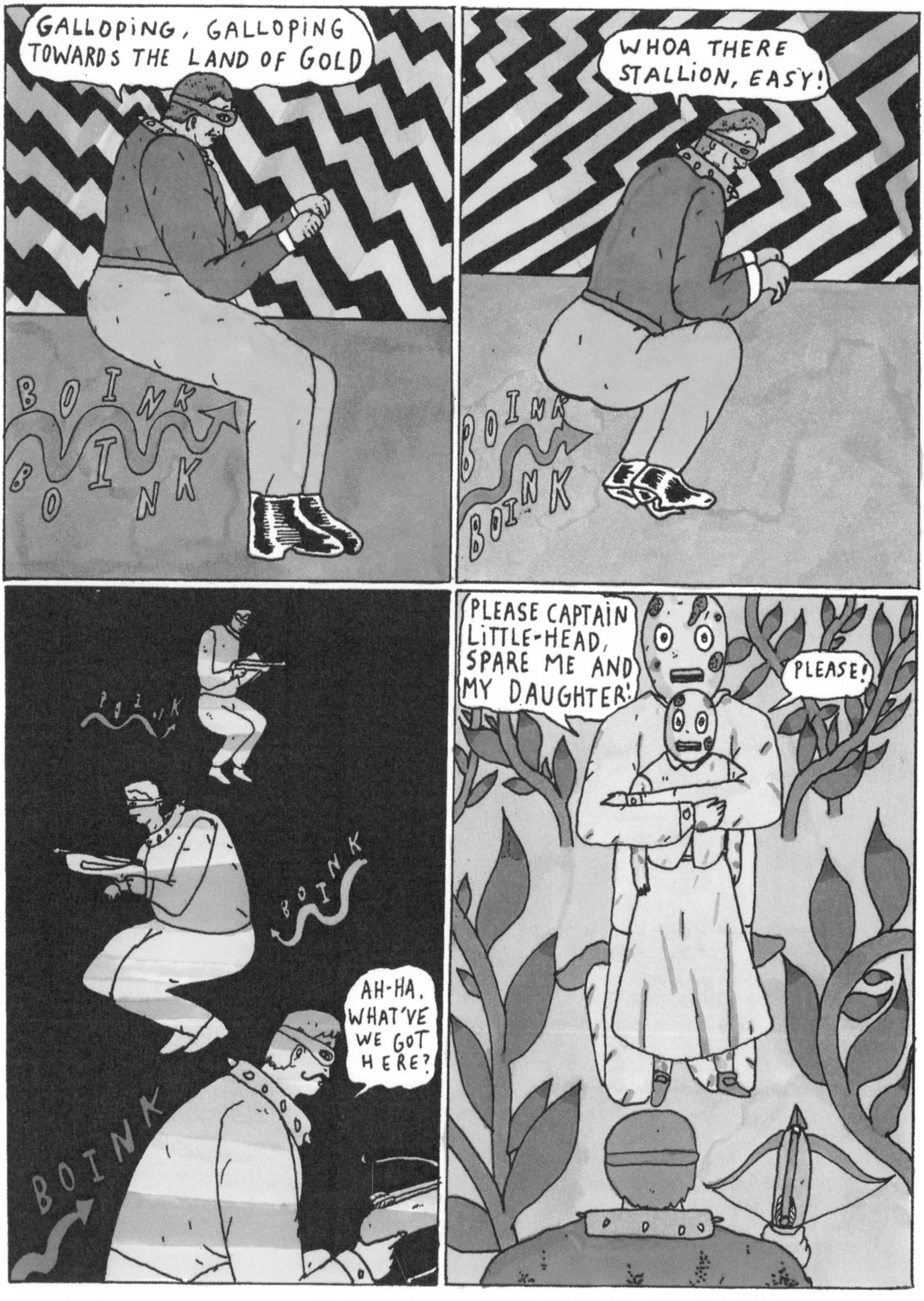
GALLOPING, GALLOPING TOWARDS THE LAND OF GOLD
BOINK
BOINK
WHOA THERE STALLION, EASY!
BOINK
BOINK
BOINK
BOINK
AH-HA. WHAT'VE WE GOT HERE?
BOINK
PLEASE CAPTAIN LITTLE-HEAD, SPARE ME AND MY DAUGHTER!
PLEASE!

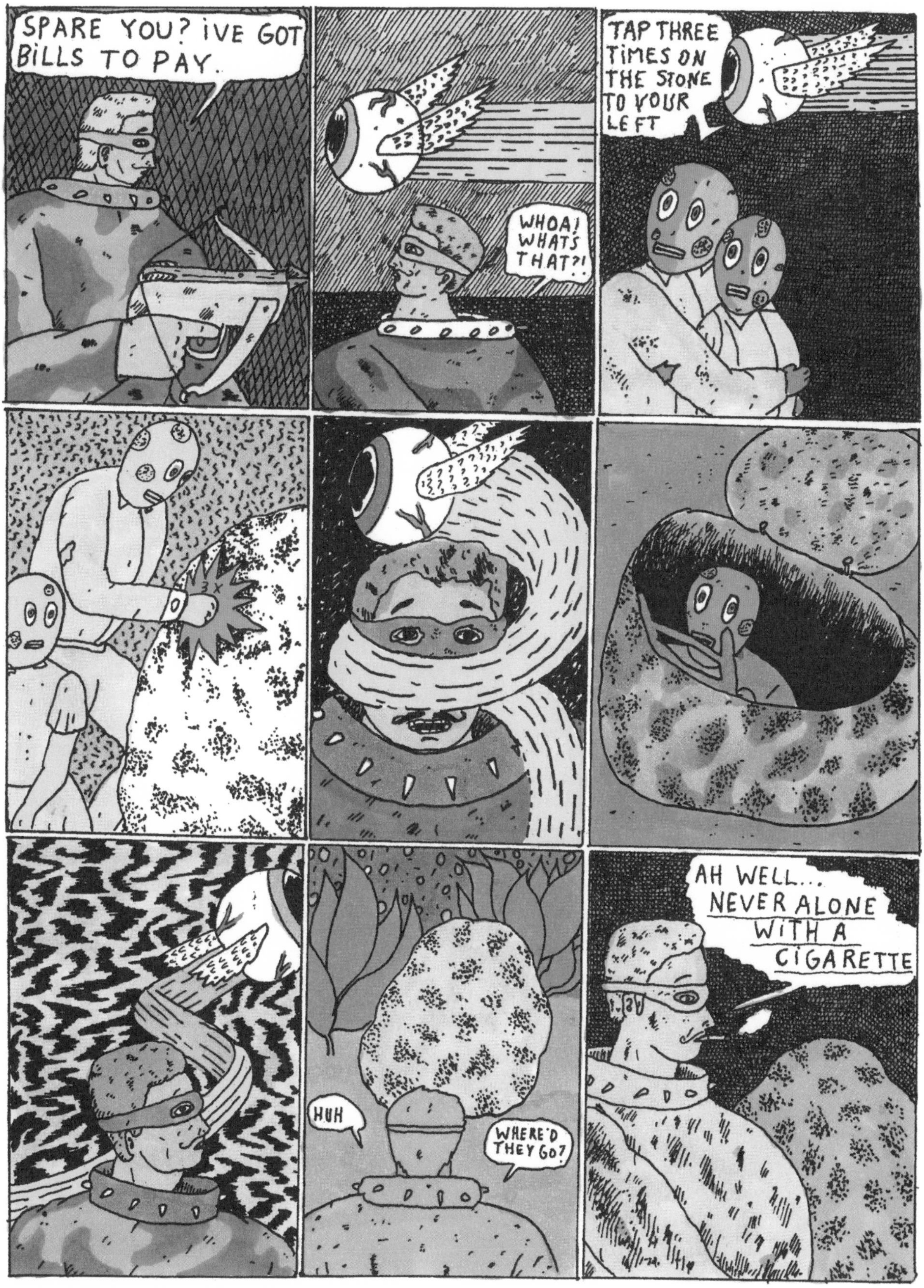
SPARE YOU? iVE GOT BiLLS TO PAY.
WHOA! WHAT'S THAT?!
TAP THREE TiMES ON THE STONE TO YOUR LEFT
3X
HUH
WHERE'D THEY GO?
AH WELL... NEVER ALONE WiTH A CiGARETTE

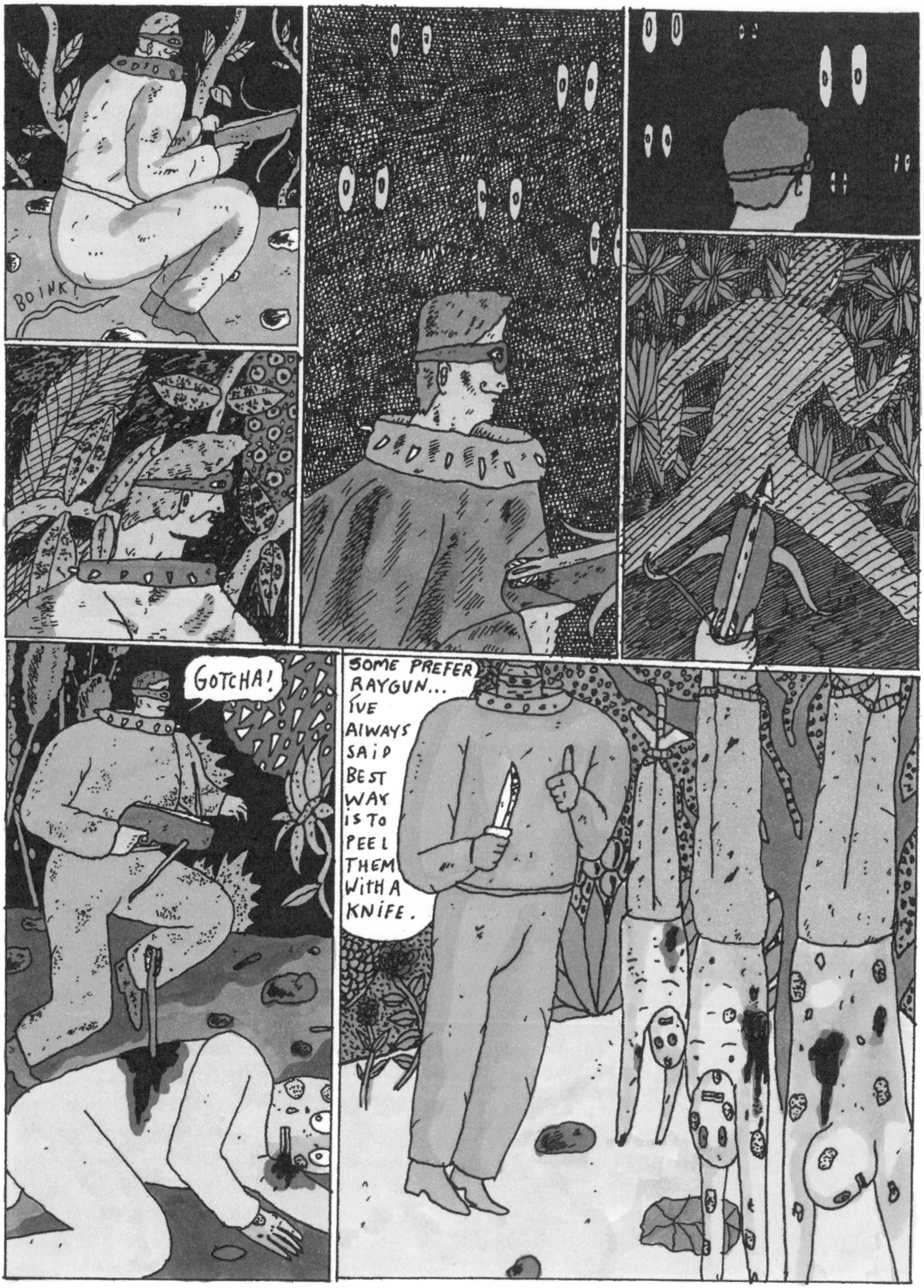
BOINK!
GOTCHA!
SOME PREFER RAYGUN... I'VE ALWAYS SAID BEST WAY IS TO PEEL THEM WITH A KNIFE.

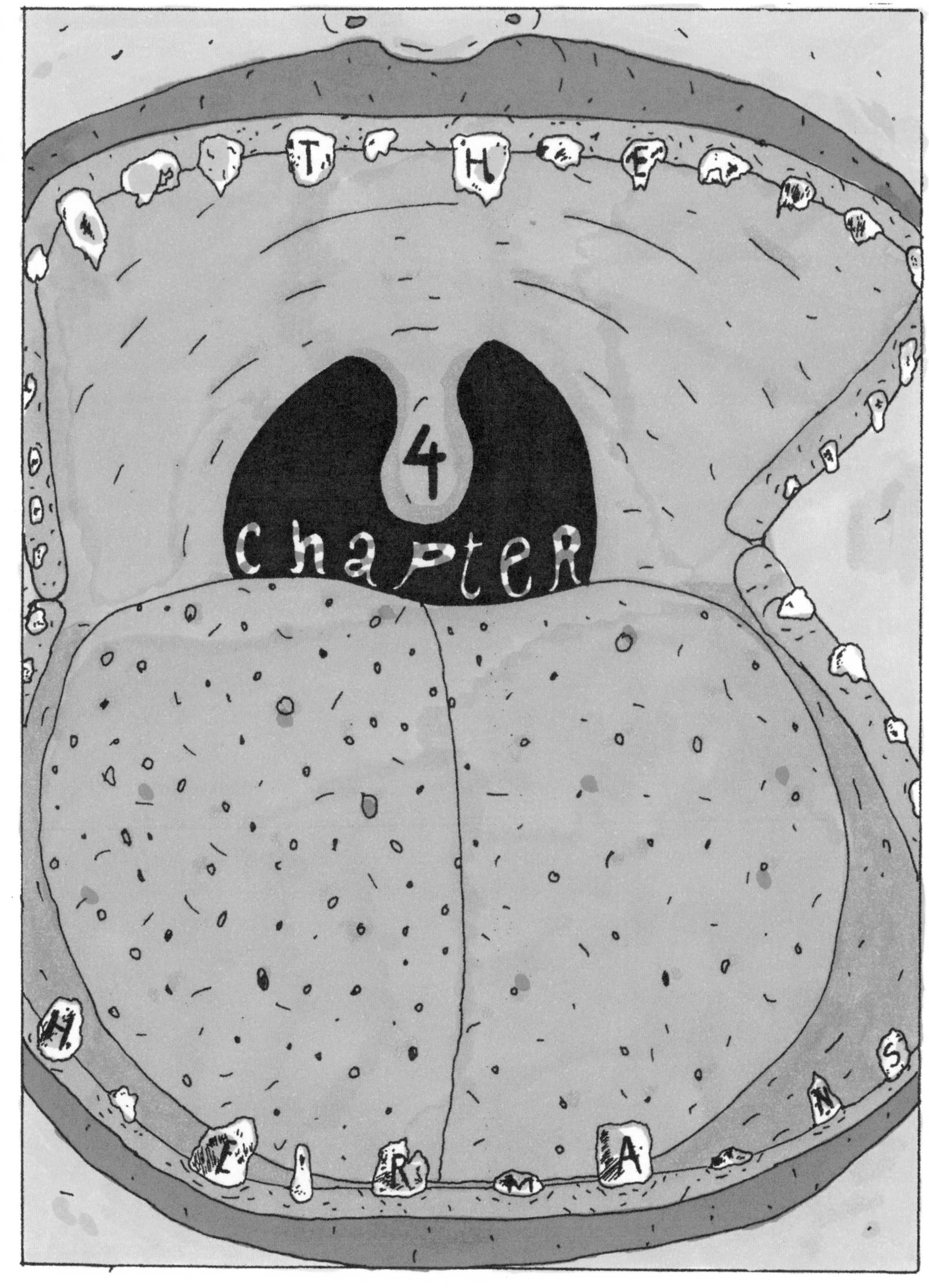
4
Chapter
THE

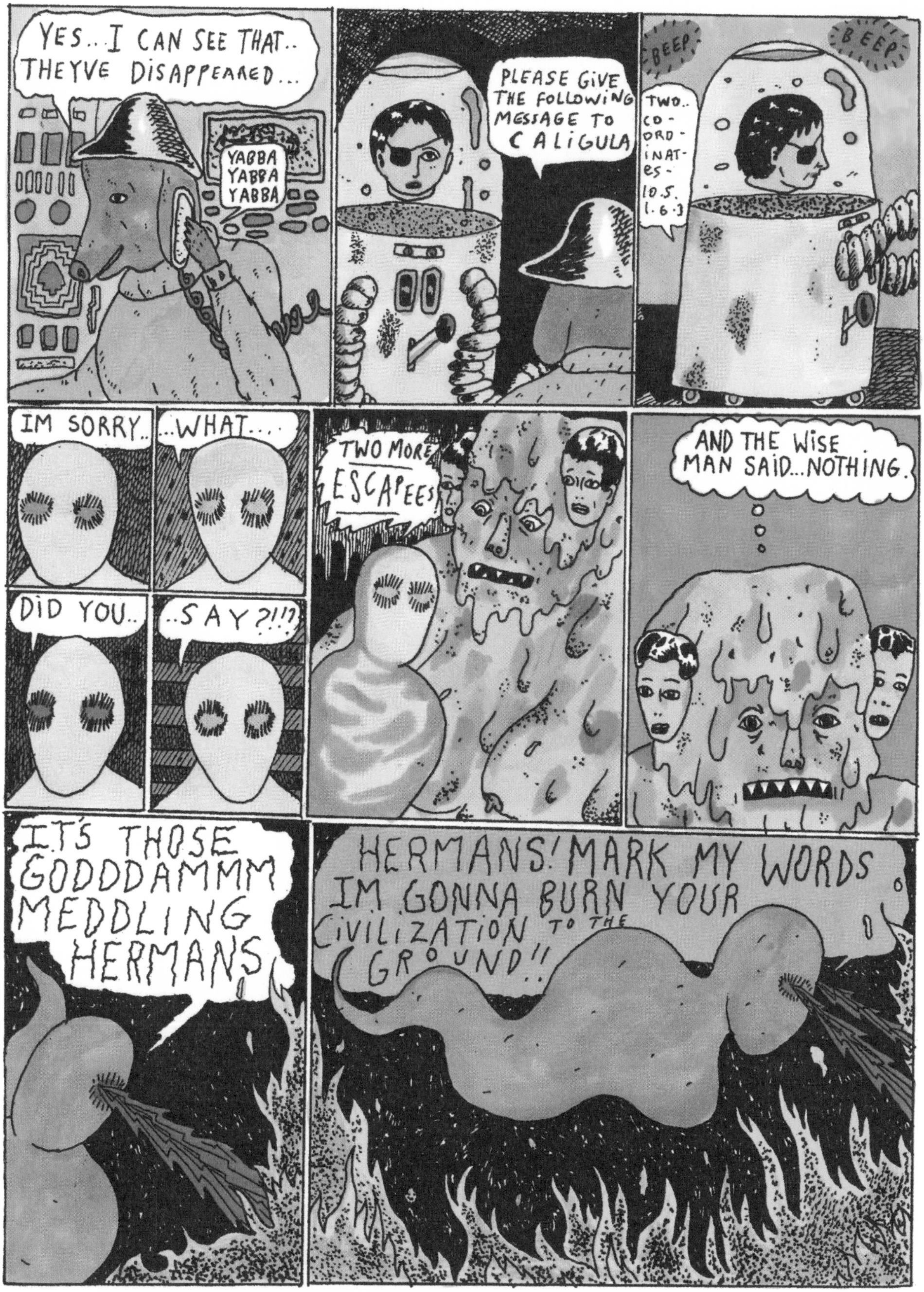
YES.. I CAN SEE THAT.. THEYVE DISAPPEARED...
YABBA YABBA YABBA
PLEASE GIVE THE FOLLOWING MESSAGE TO CALIGULA
BEEP
BEEP
TWO.. CO-ORD-INAT-ES- 10.5. 1.6.
IM SORRY..
..WHAT...
DID YOU..
..SAY?!!?
TWO MORE ESCAPEES!
AND THE WISE MAN SAID...NOTHING.
IT'S THOSE GODDDAMMM MEDDLING HERMANS
HERMANS! MARK MY WORDS IM GONNA BURN YOUR CIVILIZATION TO THE GROUND!!

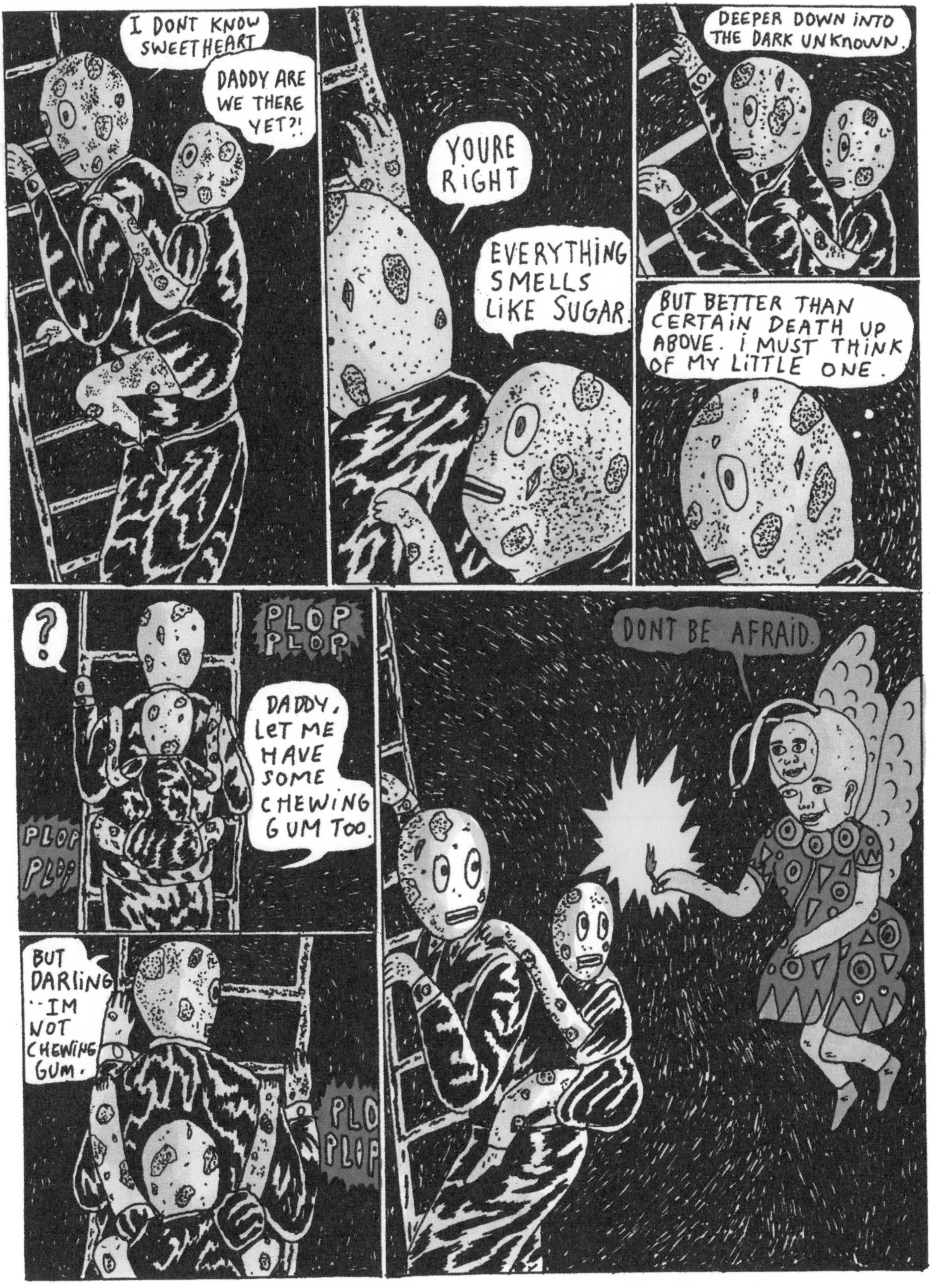

I DONT KNOW SWEETHEART
DADDY ARE WE THERE YET?!
YOURE RIGHT
EVERYTHING SMELLS LIKE SUGAR
DEEPER DOWN INTO THE DARK UNKNOWN.
BUT BETTER THAN CERTAIN DEATH UP ABOVE. I MUST THINK OF MY LITTLE ONE.
?
PLOP PLOP
DADDY, LET ME HAVE SOME CHEWING GUM TOO.
PLOP PLOP
BUT DARLING.. IM NOT CHEWING GUM.
PLO PLOP
DONT BE AFRAID.

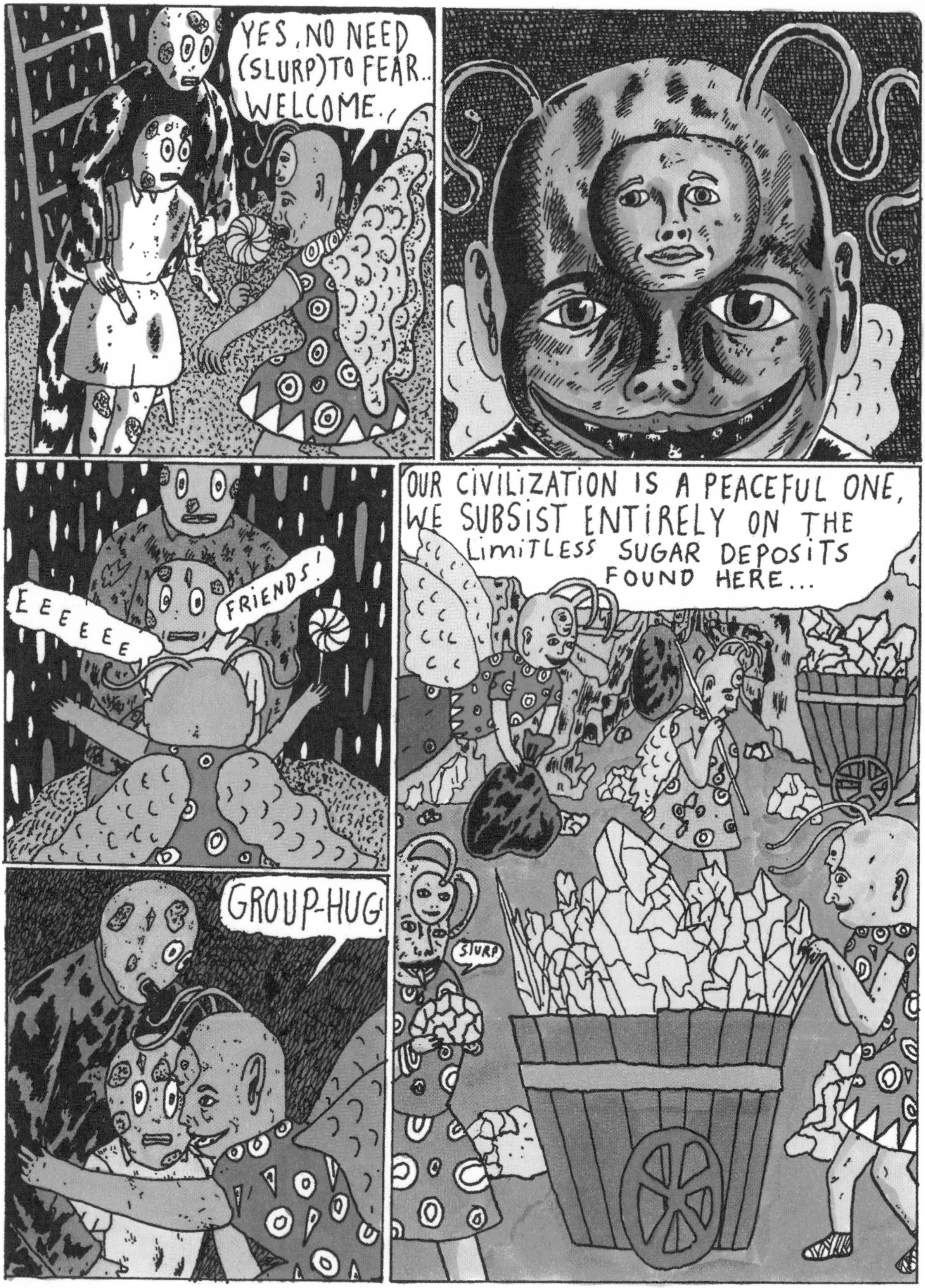
YES, NO NEED (SLURP) TO FEAR.. WELCOME.
EEEEEEE
FRIENDS!
GROUP-HUG
OUR CIVILIZATION IS A PEACEFUL ONE, WE SUBSIST ENTIRELY ON THE LIMITLESS SUGAR DEPOSITS FOUND HERE...
SLURP

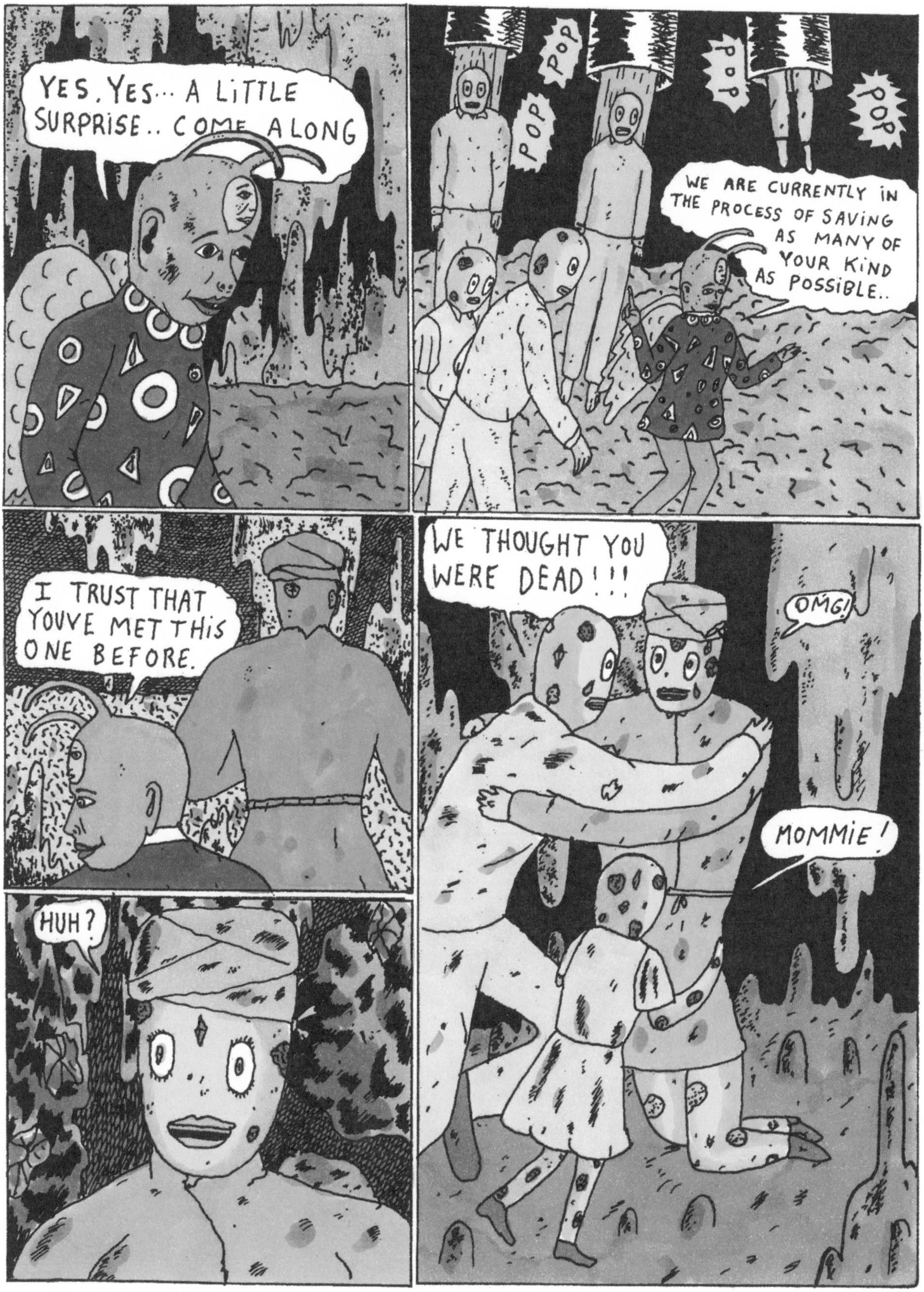
YES, YES... A LITTLE SURPRISE.. COME ALONG
POP
POP
POP
POP
WE ARE CURRENTLY IN THE PROCESS OF SAVING AS MANY OF YOUR KIND AS POSSIBLE..
I TRUST THAT YOUVE MET THIS ONE BEFORE.
HUH?
WE THOUGHT YOU WERE DEAD!!!
OMG!
MOMMIE!

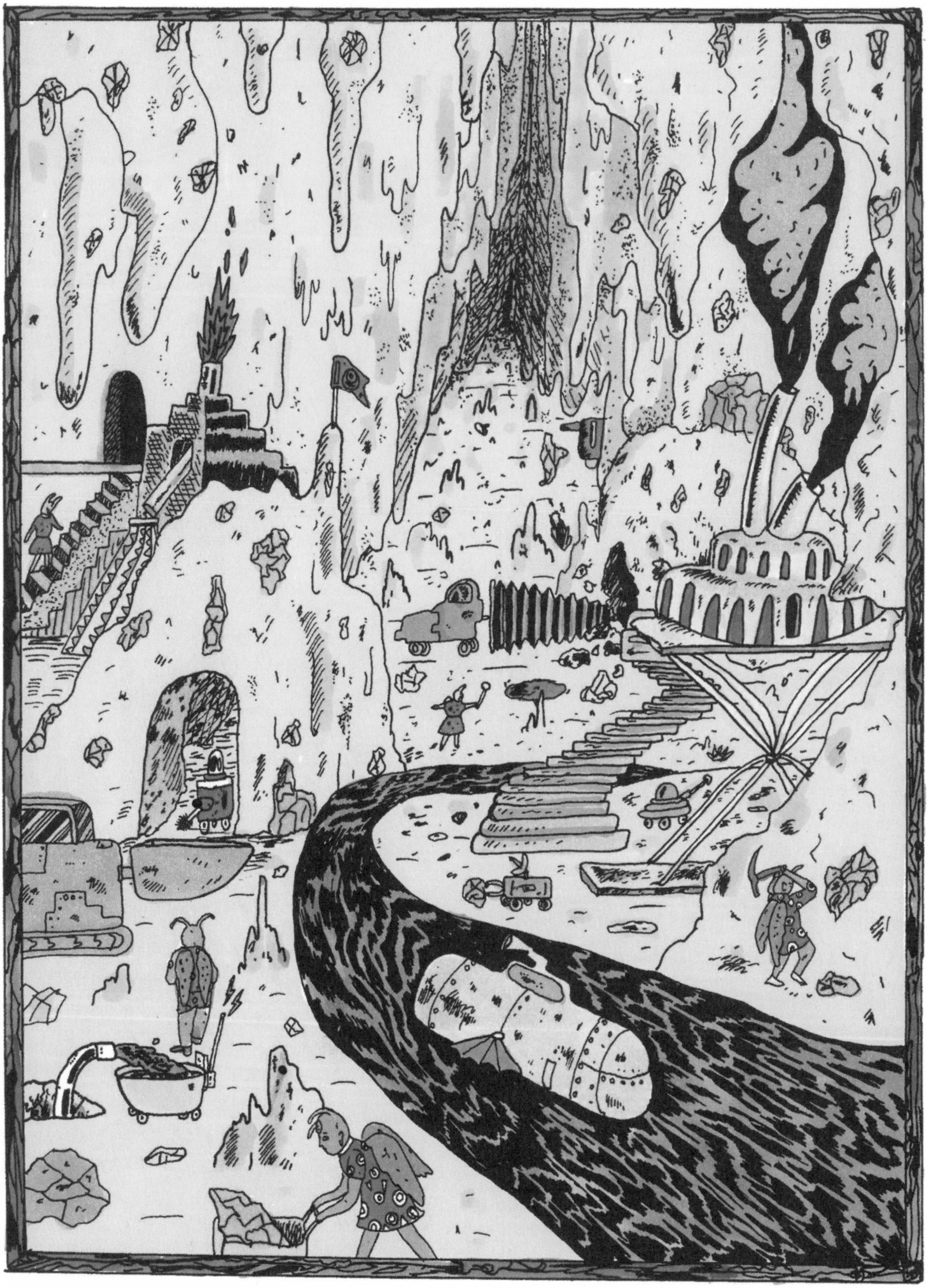

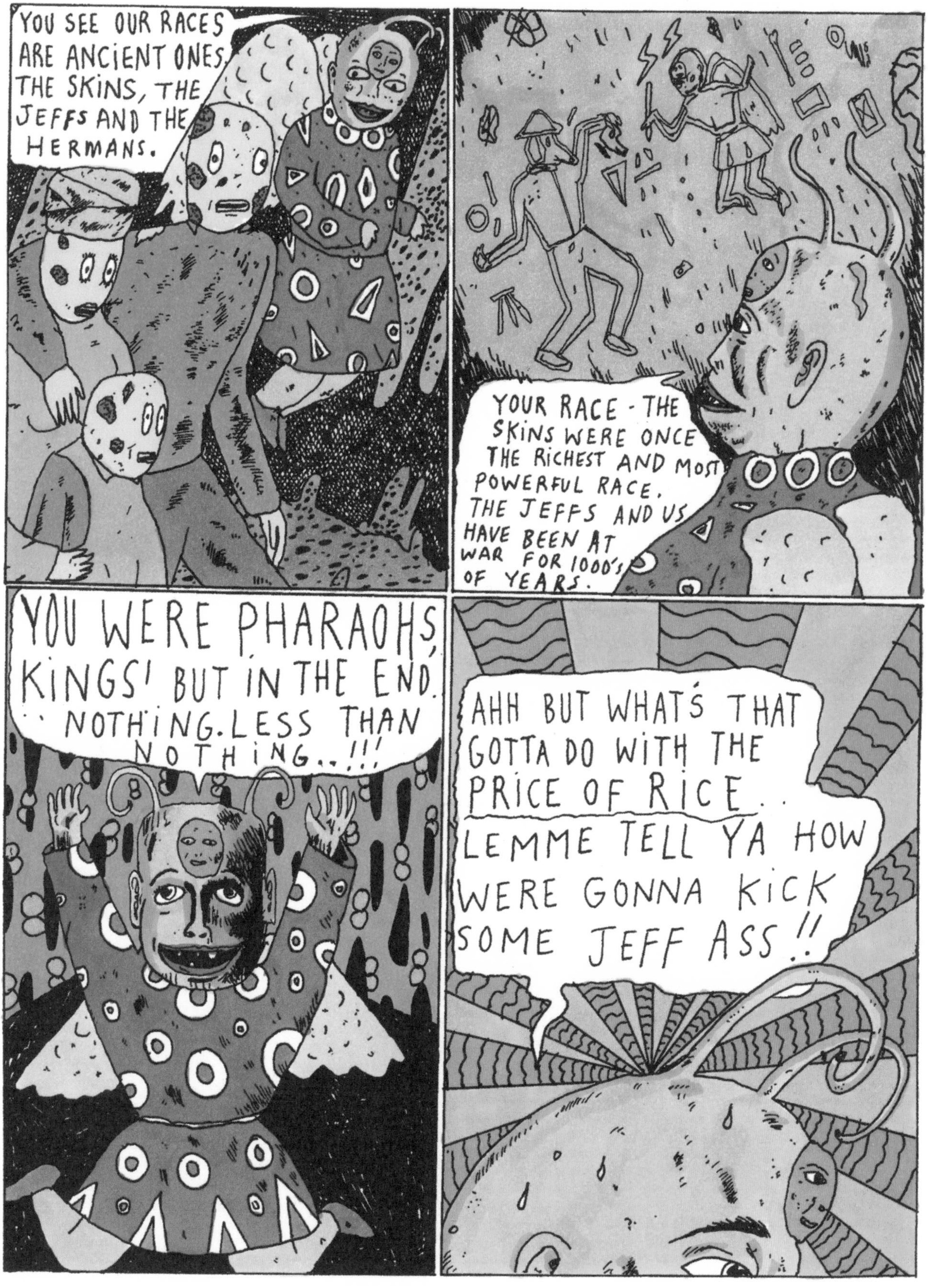
YOU SEE OUR RACES ARE ANCIENT ONES. THE SKINS, THE JEFFS AND THE HERMANS.
YOUR RACE - THE SKINS WERE ONCE THE RICHEST AND MOST POWERFUL RACE. THE JEFFS AND US HAVE BEEN AT WAR FOR 1000'S OF YEARS.
YOU WERE PHARAOHS, KINGS! BUT IN THE END NOTHING. LESS THAN NOTHING..!!!
AHH BUT WHAT'S THAT GOTTA DO WITH THE PRICE OF RICE. LEMME TELL YA HOW WERE GONNA KICK SOME JEFF ASS!!

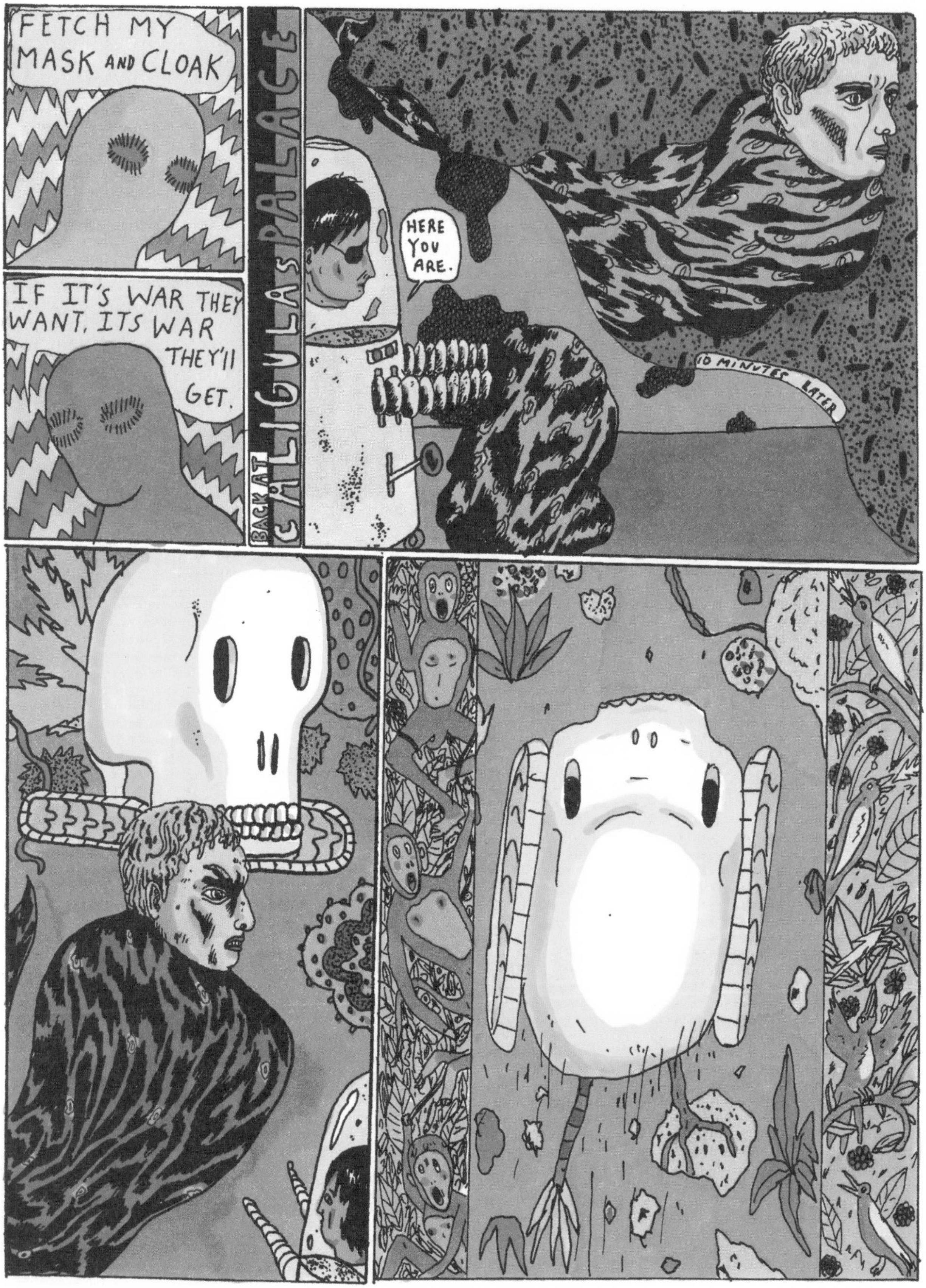
FETCH MY MASK AND CLOAK
IF IT'S WAR THEY WANT, ITS WAR THEY'll GET.
BACK AT CALIGULAS PALACE
HERE YOU ARE.
10 MINUTES LATER

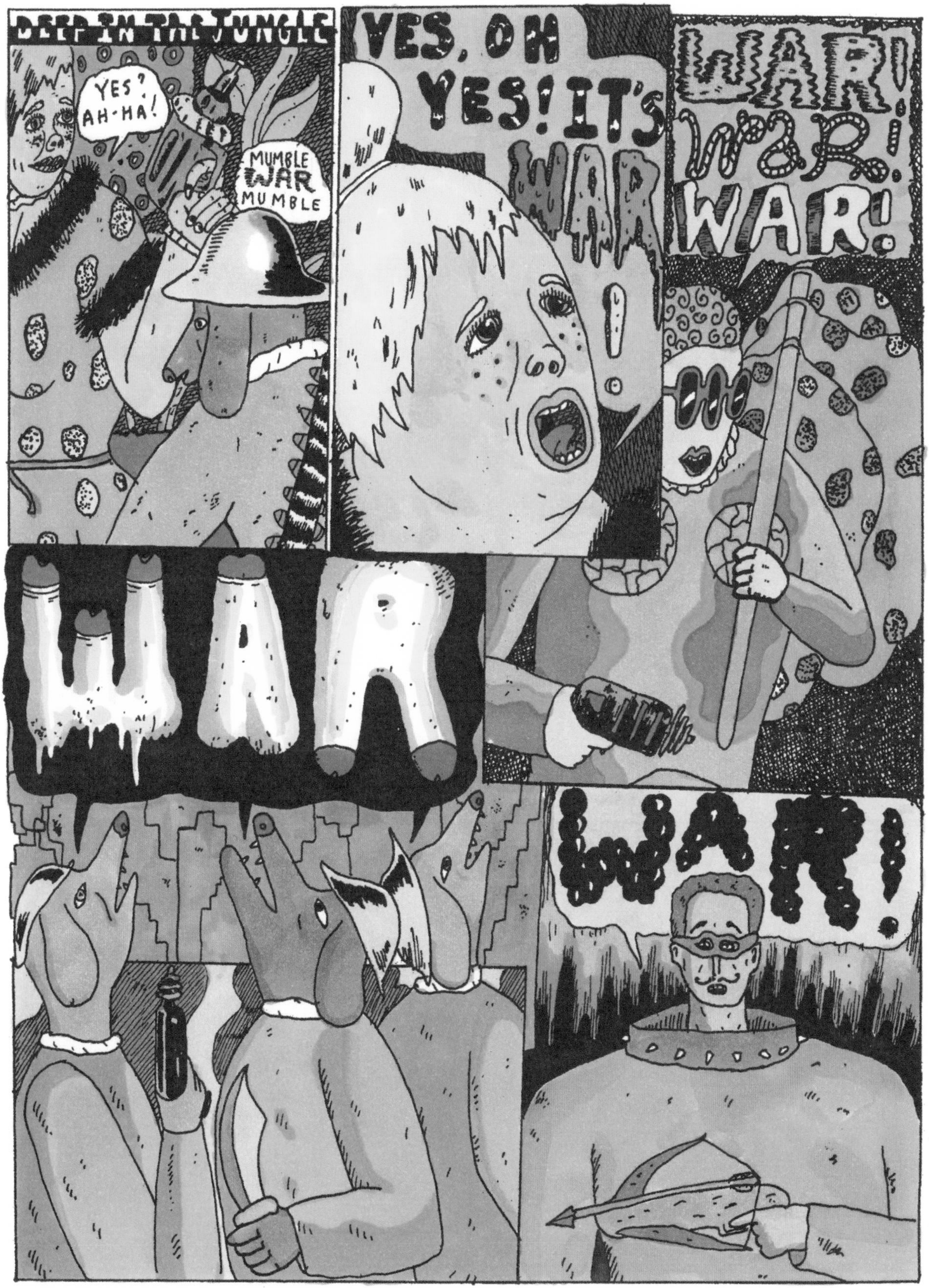
DEEP IN THE JUNGLE
YES? AH-HA!
MUMBLE WAR MUMBLE
YES, OH YES! IT'S WAR!
WAR! WAR! WAR!
WAR
WAR!

THE WAR OF THE FLOWERS

HERE ON THIS STRANGE PLANET INHABITED BY THE HERMANS AND JEFFS (AND THEIR MASTER CALIGULA) CONFLICTS OF INTEREST ARE SOLVED IN A GRAND TOURNAMENT KNOWN AS 'THE WAR OF THE FLOWERS'. EACH SIDE USES TELEPATHIC MIND CONTROL TO INFLUENCE THE FLORA AND FAUNA OF A SECTION OF THE SURROUNDING

JUNGLE. FUNGHI AGAINST FUNGHI, SNAKE AGAINST SNAKE, TREE AGAINST SMOTHERING VINE UNTIL THERE IS NOTHING LEFT ALIVE WITHIN THE PARAMETER OF THE TOURNAMENT EXCEPT THAT BELONGING TO THE VICTOR. THE STAKES ARE HIGH (HIGHER THAN THEY'VE EVER BEEN) THE BRAVE AND NOBLE HERMANS

ARE WILLING TO SACRIFICE HALF OF THEIR SUGAR MINE TO CALIGULA IF THEY LOSE- IF THEY WIN THE SKINS ARE TO BE SET FREE AND 'THE HUNT' TO BE CALLED OFF PERMANENTLY.... WITH THEIR LIVES HANGING IN THE BALANCE THERE IS SIMPLY NOTHING FOR THE SKINS TO DO BUT WAIT.....

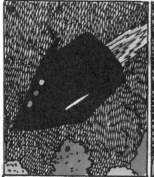

MORE GUESTS ARRIVE

LOCAL DIGNITARIES

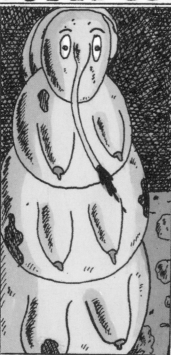

SOME WELL KNOWN CELEBRITIES DRESSED IN THE HEIGHT OF HAUTE COUTURE.

PLUS A TON OF LIVE ACTS INCLUDING THE ALL JEFF BOYBAND "JEFF ZONE" PERFORMING THEIR SUPER HIT "TRACTOR-BEAM MAMMA".

IT IS NEARLY IMPOSSIBLE TO CONTAIN THE EXCITEMENT.

FOR SOME IT IS CLEARLY THE BEST DAY OF THEIR LIVES.

OMG, ITS REALLY HIM!

FOR OTHERS....NOT SO MUCH.

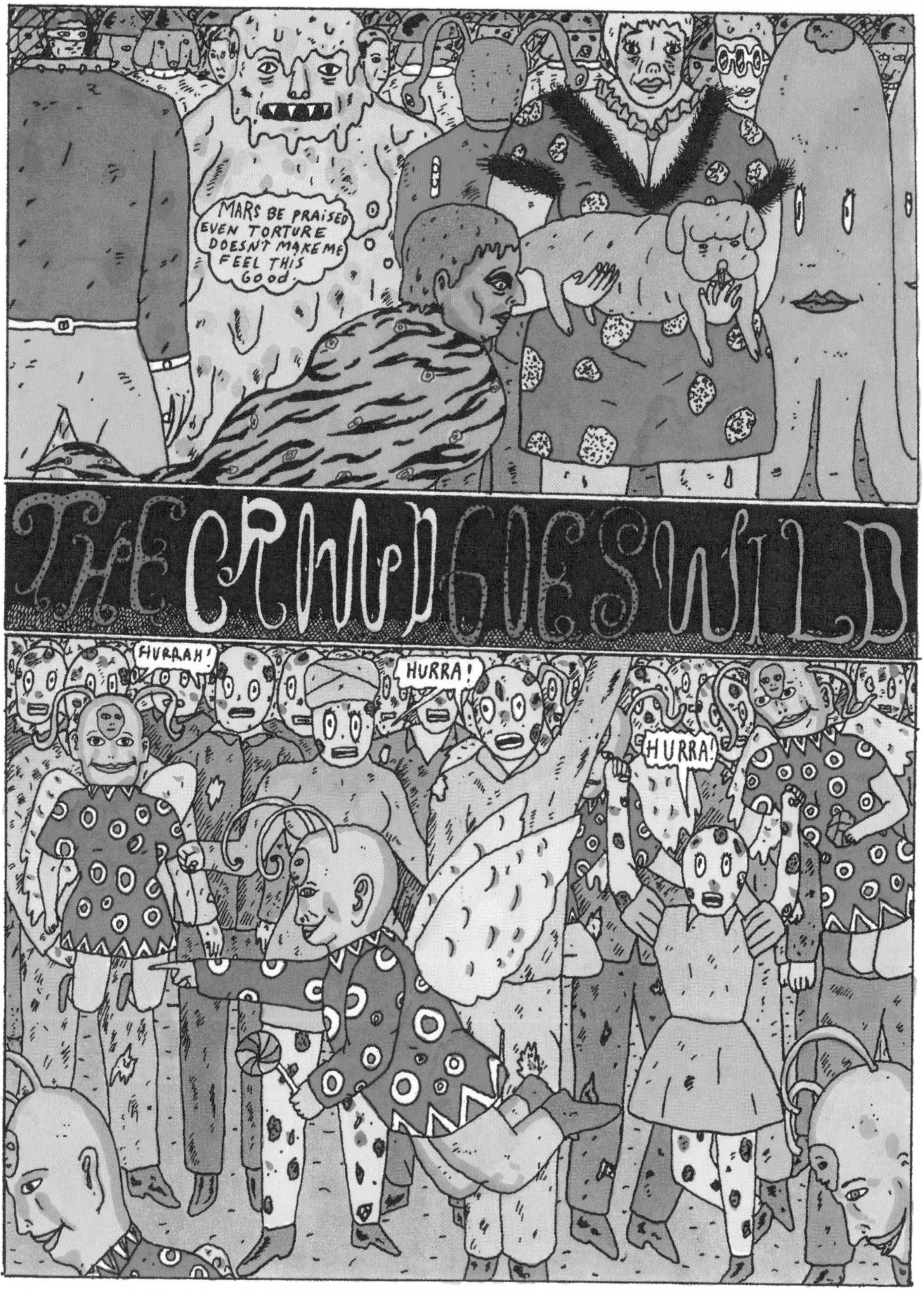
MARS BE PRAISED EVEN TORTURE DOESN'T MAKE ME FEEL THIS GOOD.
THE CROWD GOES WILD
HURRAH!
HURRA!
HURRA!

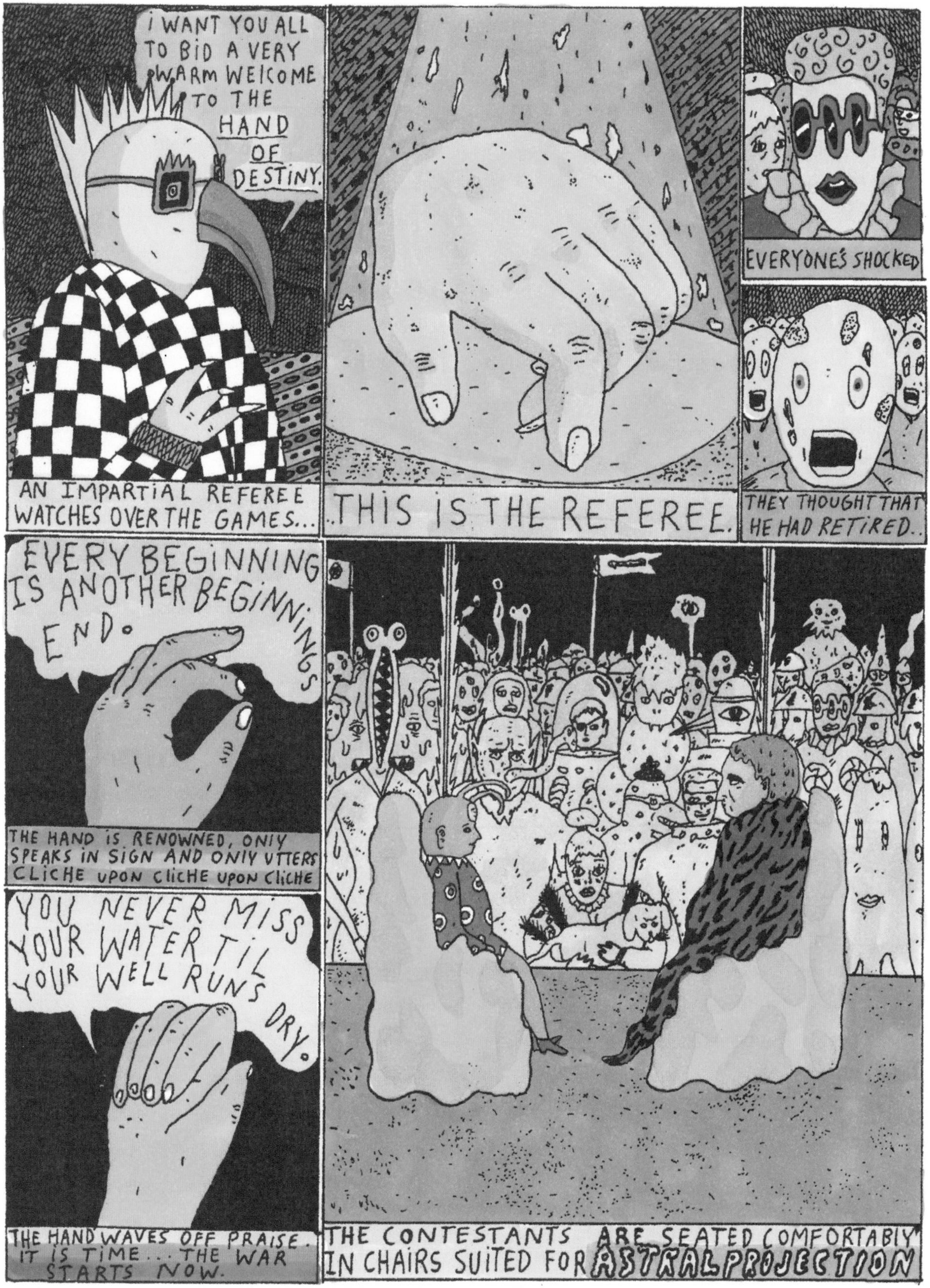

I WANT YOU ALL TO BID A VERY WARM WELCOME TO THE HAND OF DESTINY.
AN IMPARTIAL REFEREE WATCHES OVER THE GAMES...
THIS IS THE REFEREE.
EVERYONE'S SHOCKED
THEY THOUGHT THAT HE HAD RETIRED..
EVERY BEGINNING IS ANOTHER BEGINNINGS END.
THE HAND IS RENOWNED, ONLY SPEAKS IN SIGN AND ONLY UTTERS CLICHE UPON CLICHE UPON CLICHE
YOU NEVER MISS YOUR WATER TIL YOUR WELL RUNS DRY.
THE HAND WAVES OFF PRAISE. IT IS TIME.. THE WAR STARTS NOW.
THE CONTESTANTS ARE SEATED COMFORTABLY IN CHAIRS SUITED FOR ASTRAL PROJECTION

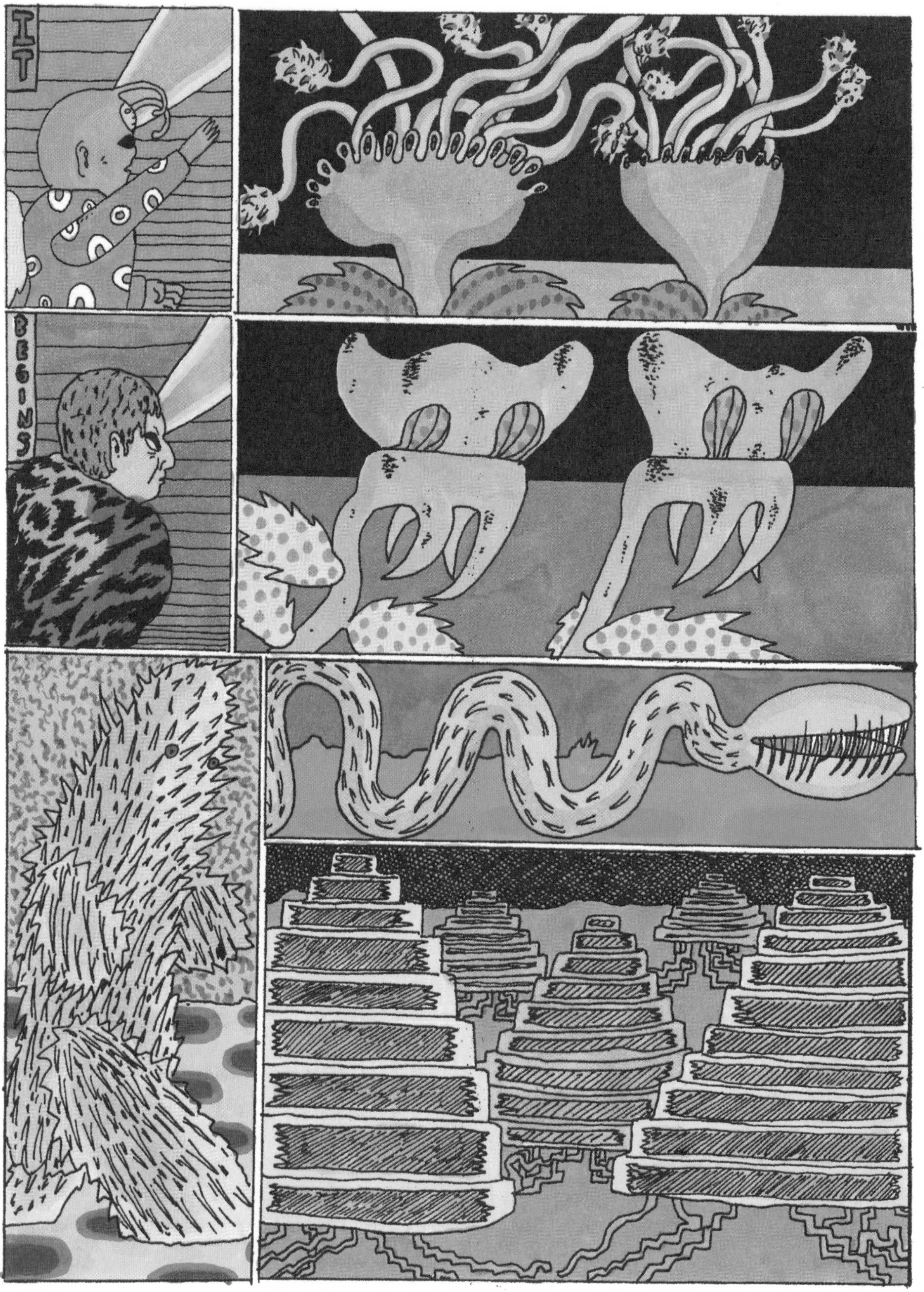
IT
BEGINS

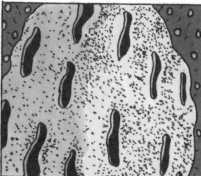

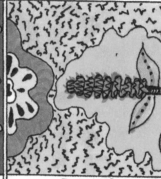

MESSAGES ARE TRANSMITTED

AND RECEIVED -

FLORAL SEMAPHORES,

MICRO PARTICLES .

ELABORATE DANCING AND

SPORES.

READY....AIM...

BALLISTICS OF PSYCHOTROPIC TOXINS ARE FIRED

DISEASE SPREADS AMONGST THE ENEMY

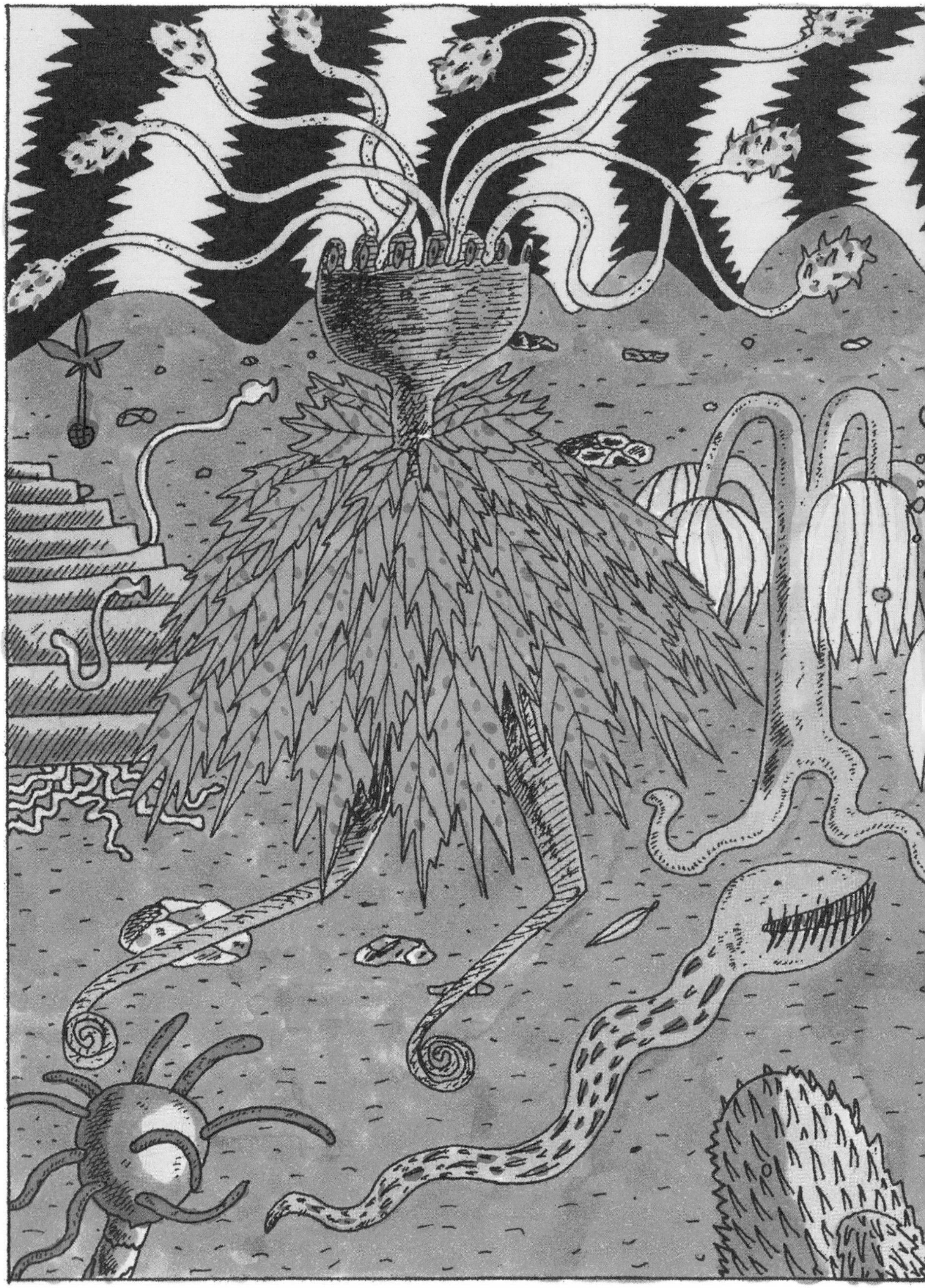

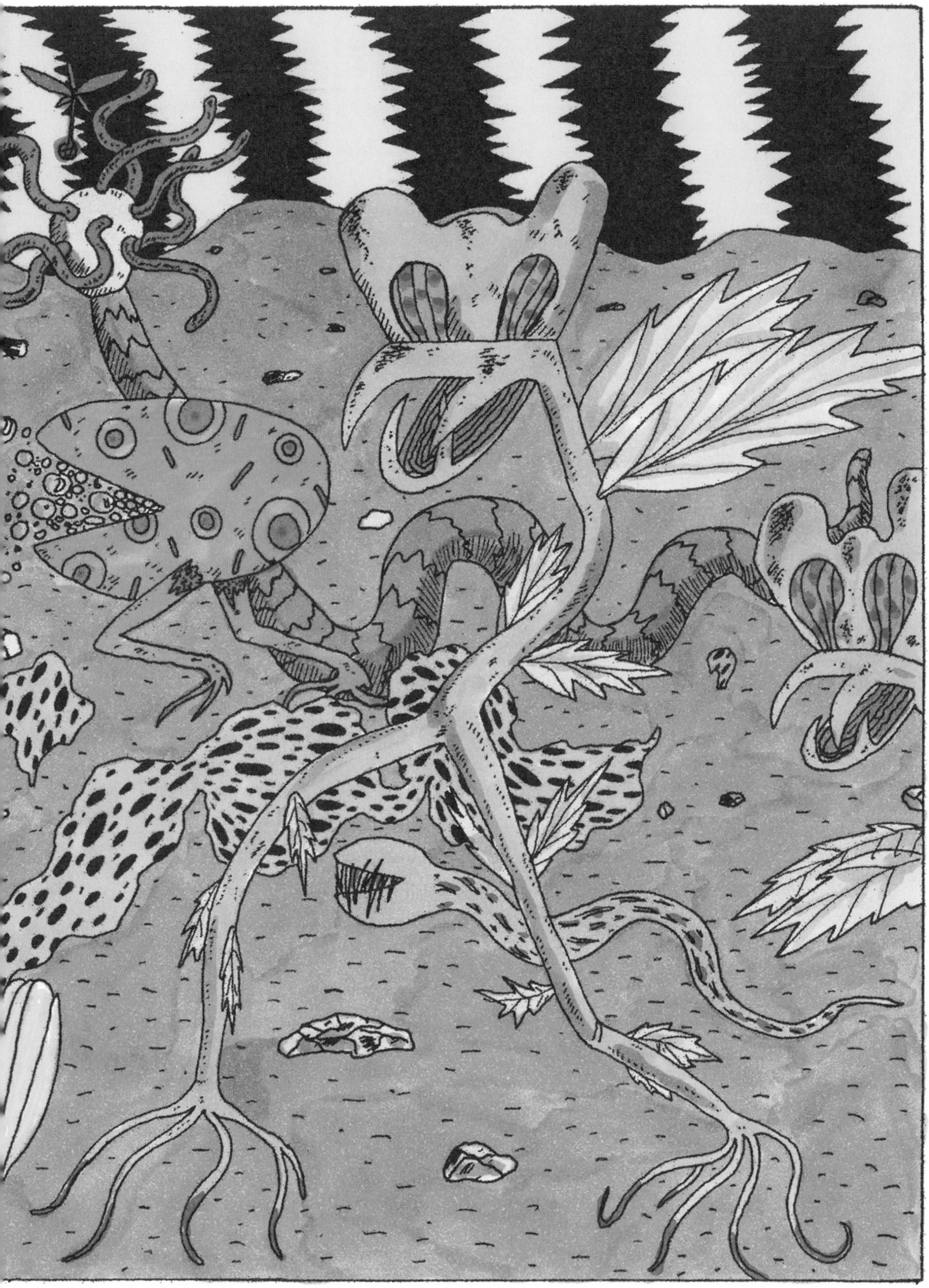

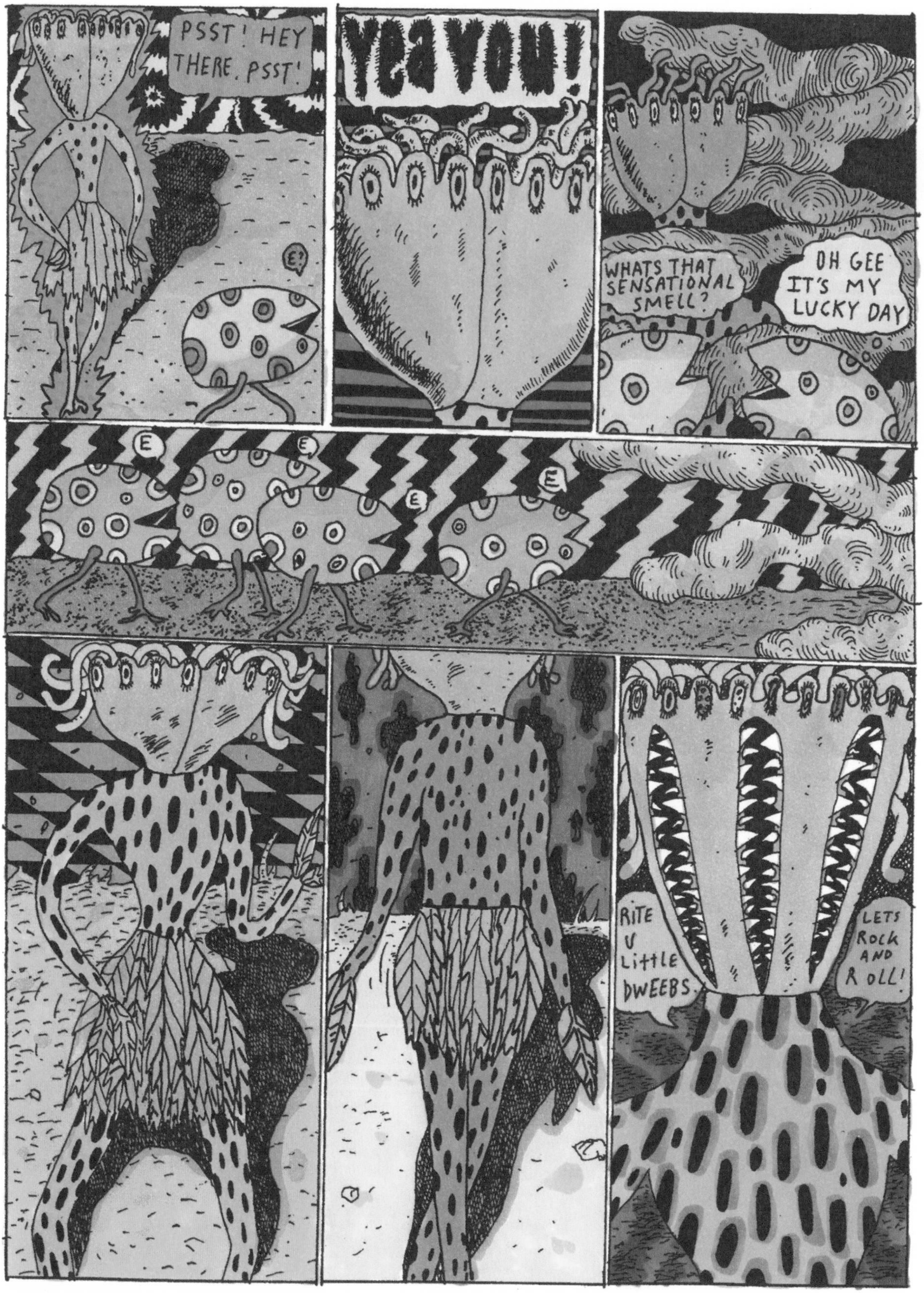
PSST! HEY THERE. PSST!
E?
YEA YOU!
WHATS THAT SENSATIONAL SMELL?
OH GEE IT'S MY LUCKY DAY
E
E
E
E
RITE U LITTLE DWEEBS.
LETS ROCK AND ROLL!

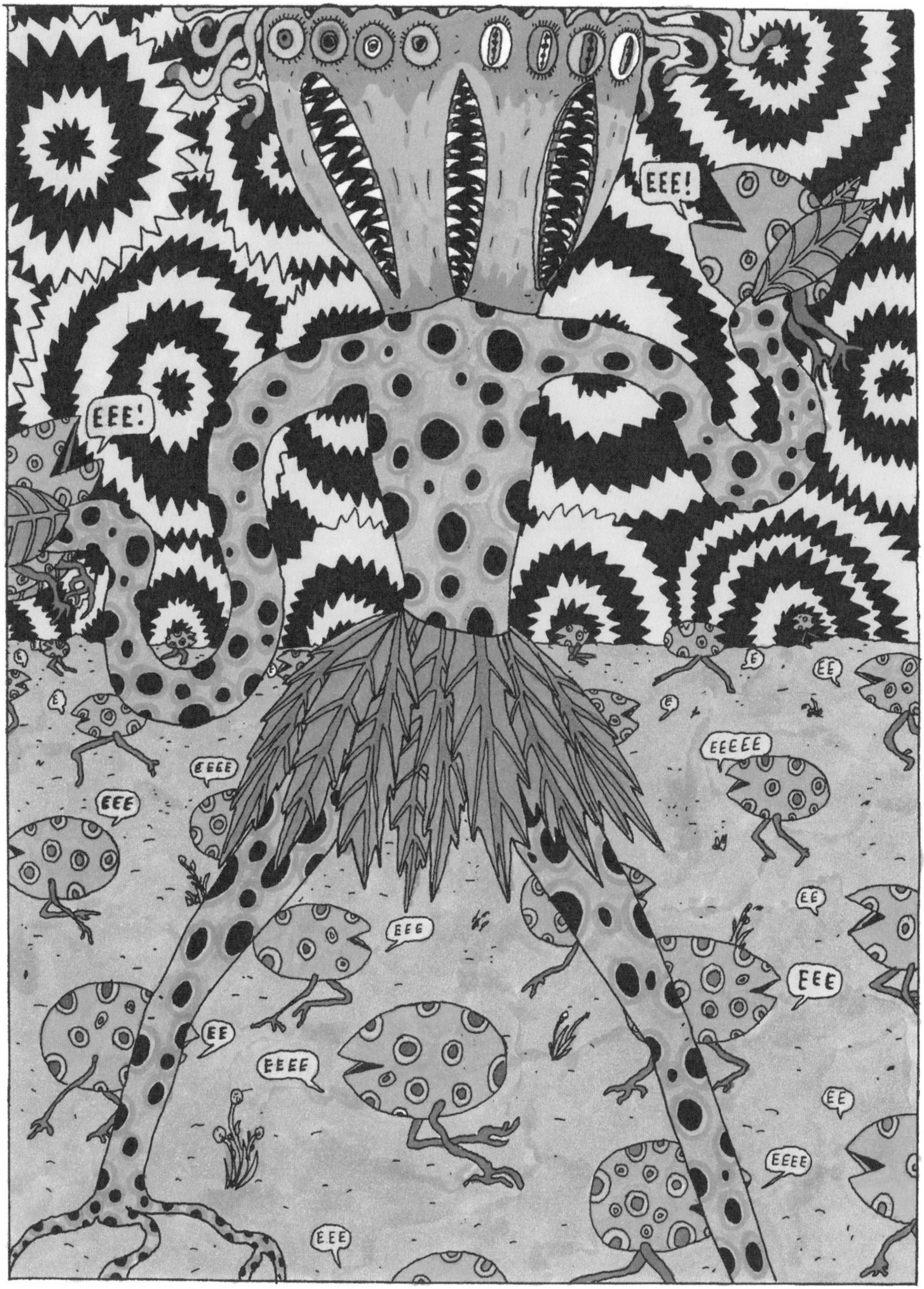
EEE!
EEE!
EEEEE
EEEE
EEE
EE
EEE
EEE
EE
EEEE
EE
EEEE
EEE

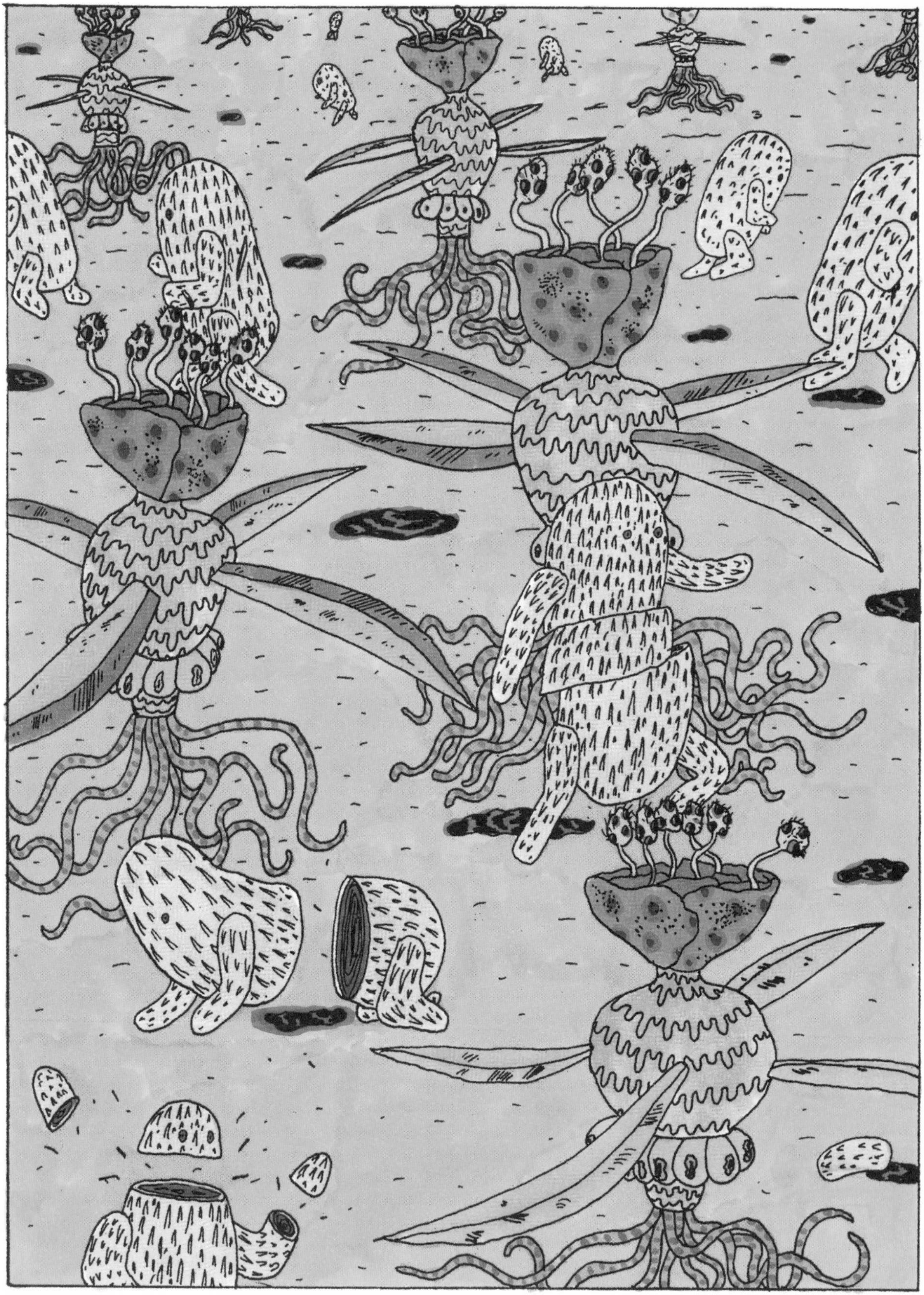

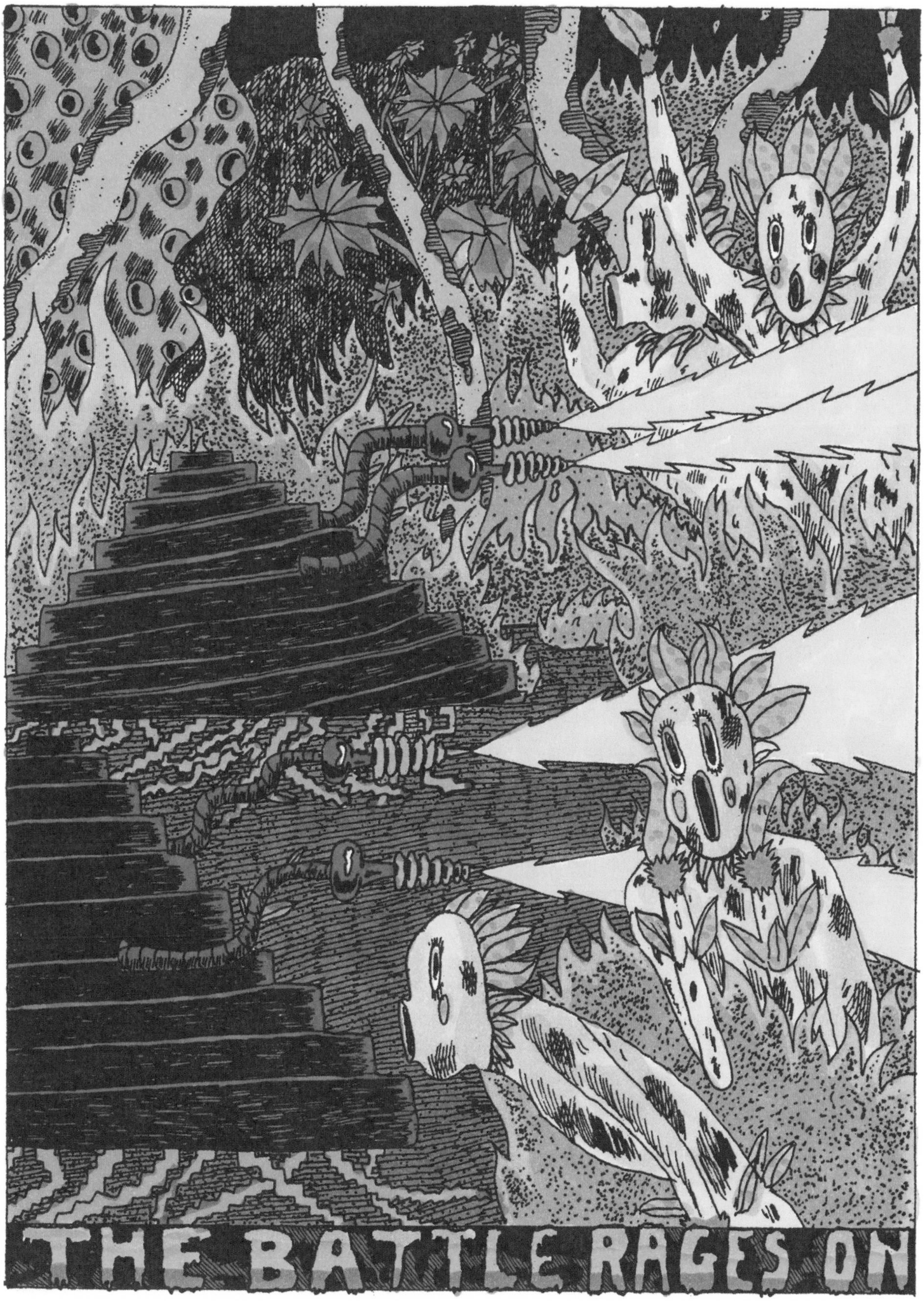

THE BATTLE RAGES ON

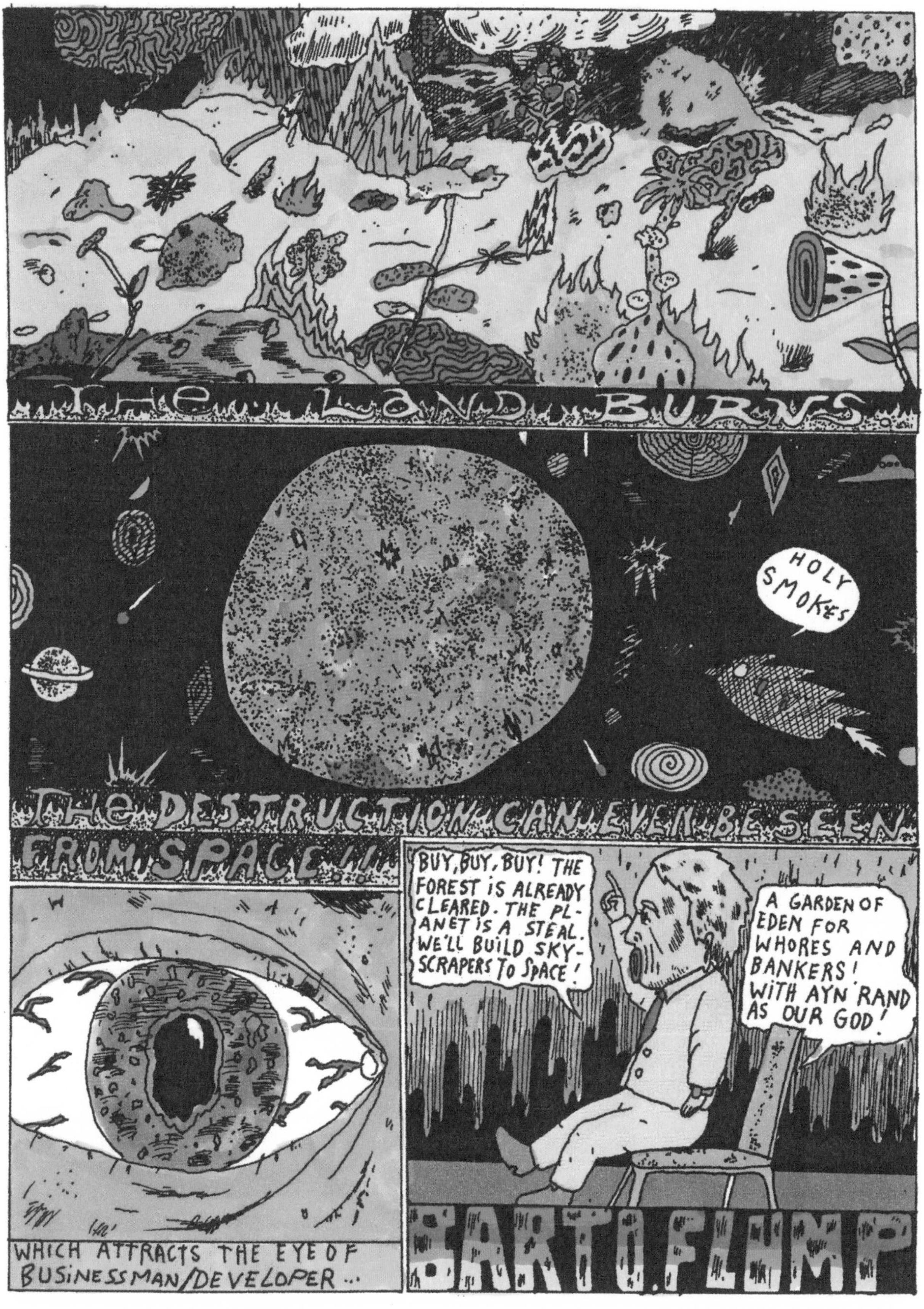
THE LAND BURNS.
HOLY SMOKES
THE DESTRUCTION CAN EVEN BE SEEN FROM SPACE!!
WHICH ATTRACTS THE EYE OF BUSINESSMAN/DEVELOPER...
BUY, BUY, BUY! THE FOREST IS ALREADY CLEARED. THE PLANET IS A STEAL. WE'LL BUILD SKYSCRAPERS TO SPACE!
A GARDEN OF EDEN FOR WHORES AND BANKERS! WITH AYN RAND AS OUR GOD!
BARTO FLUMP

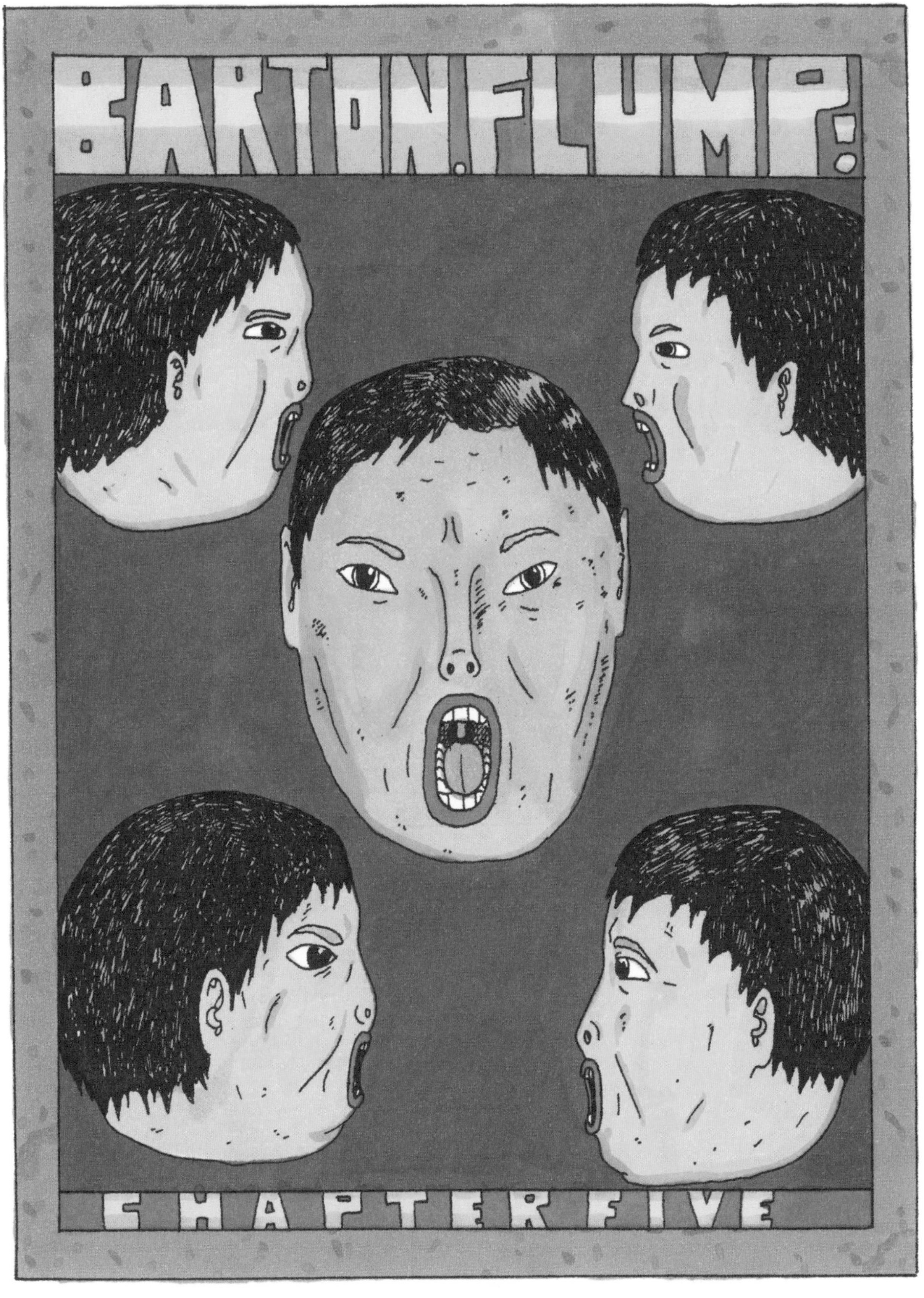
BARTON.FLUMP?!
CHAPTER FIVE

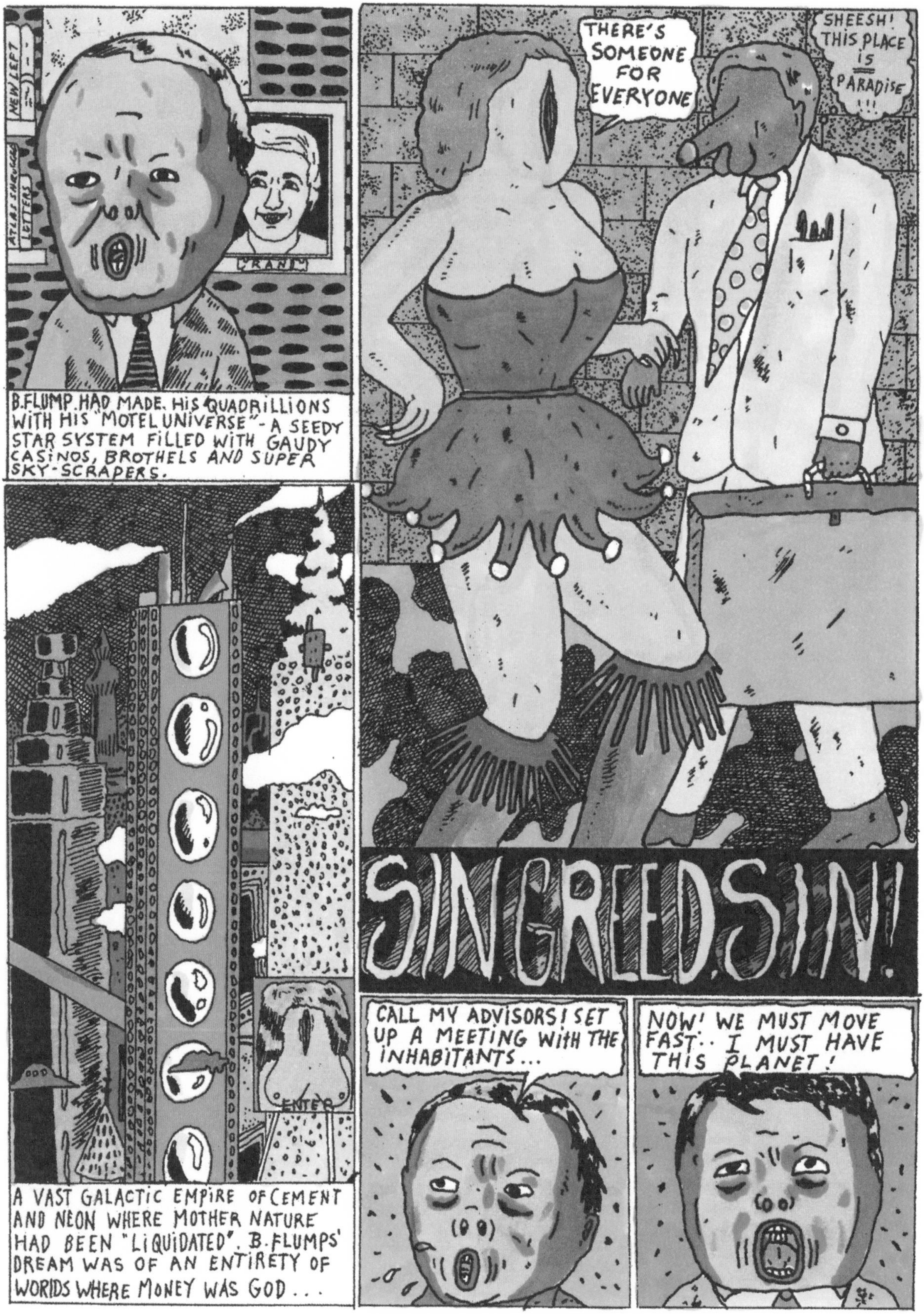
NEW LEFT
ATLAS SHRUGGED
LETTERS
RAND
B.FLUMP HAD MADE HIS QUADRILLIONS WITH HIS "MOTEL UNIVERSE" - A SEEDY STAR SYSTEM FILLED WITH GAUDY CASINOS, BROTHELS AND SUPER SKY-SCRAPERS.
THERE'S SOMEONE FOR EVERYONE
SHEESH! THIS PLACE IS PARADISE !!!
ENTER
SIN.GREED.SIN!
A VAST GALACTIC EMPIRE OF CEMENT AND NEON WHERE MOTHER NATURE HAD BEEN "LIQUIDATED". B.FLUMPS' DREAM WAS OF AN ENTIRETY OF WORLDS WHERE MONEY WAS GOD...
CALL MY ADVISORS! SET UP A MEETING WITH THE INHABITANTS...
NOW! WE MUST MOVE FAST.. I MUST HAVE THIS PLANET!

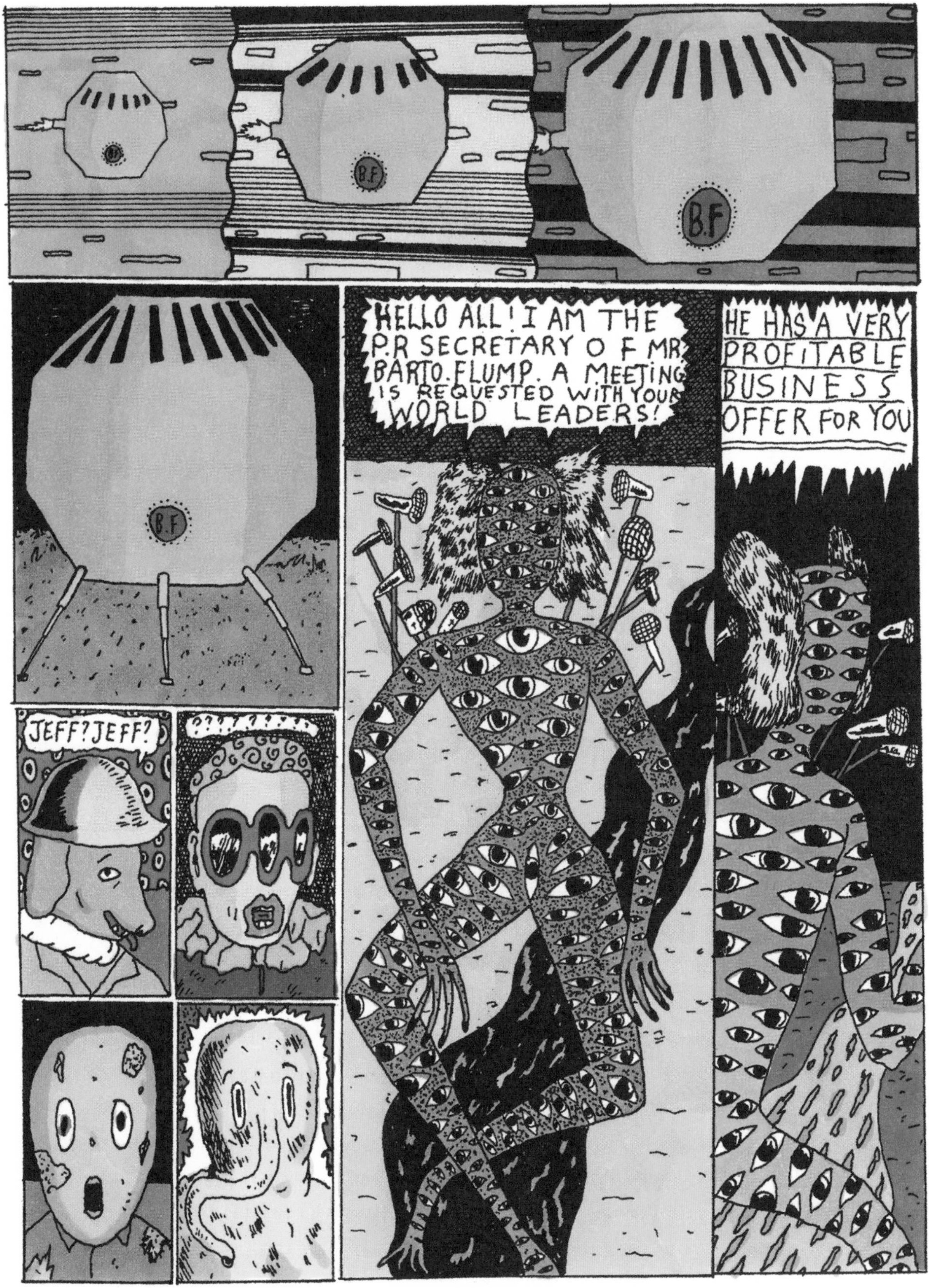
B.F
B.F
B.F
B.F
JEFF? JEFF?
HELLO ALL! I AM THE P.R SECRETARY OF MR BARTO.FLUMP. A MEETING IS REQUESTED WITH YOUR WORLD LEADERS!
HE HAS A VERY PROFITABLE BUSINESS OFFER FOR YOU

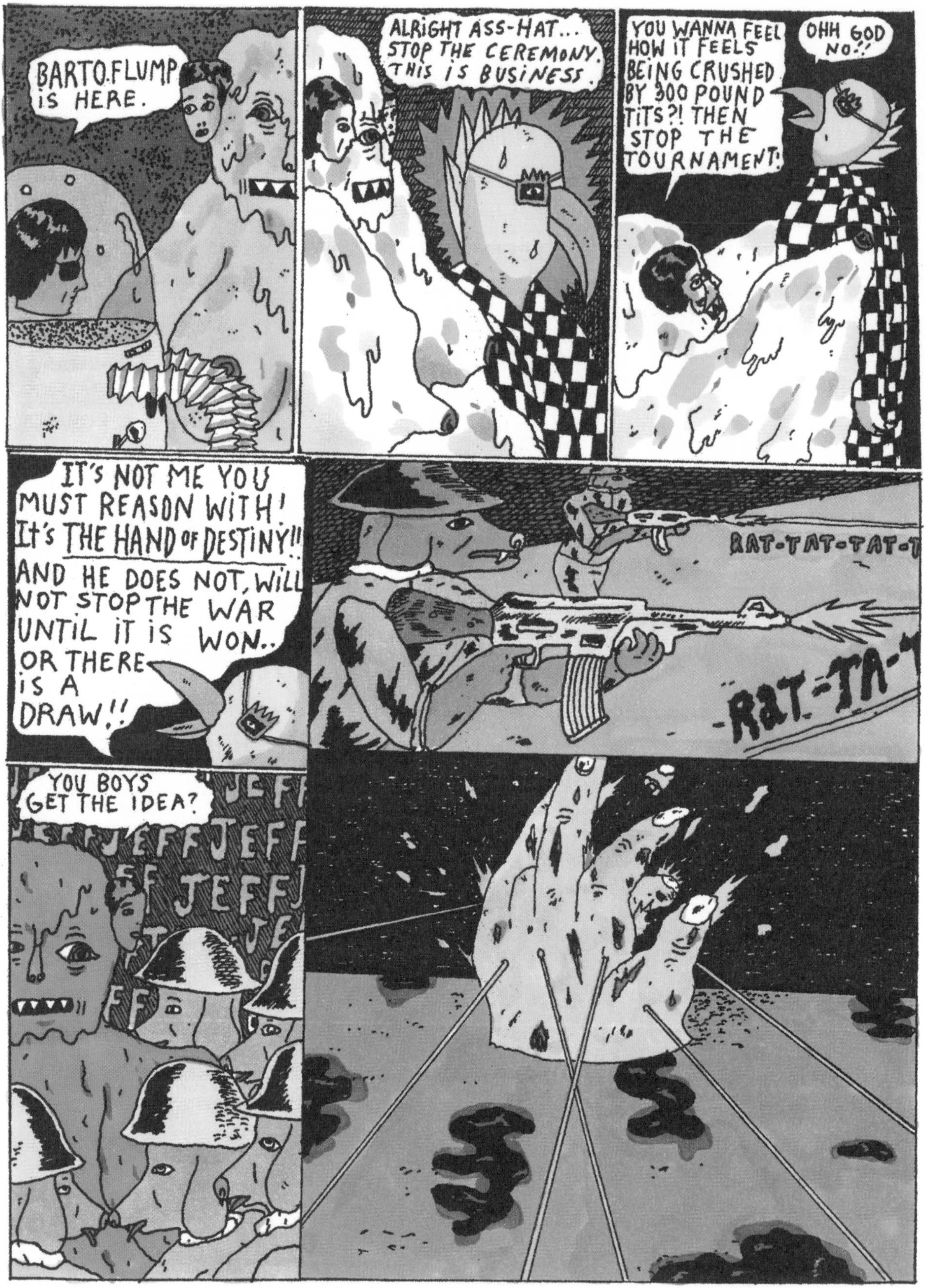
BARTO.FLUMP is HERE.
ALRIGHT ASS-HAT... STOP THE CEREMONY. THIS IS BUSINESS.
YOU WANNA FEEL HOW IT FEELS BEING CRUSHED BY 300 POUND TITS?! THEN STOP THE TOURNAMENT!
OHH GOD NO!!
IT'S NOT ME YOU MUST REASON WITH! It's THE HAND OF DESTINY!! AND HE DOES NOT, WILL NOT STOP THE WAR UNTIL IT IS WON.. OR THERE is A DRAW!!
RAT-TAT-TAT-T
-RAT-TA-
YOU BOYS GET THE IDEA?
JEFF JEFF JEFF

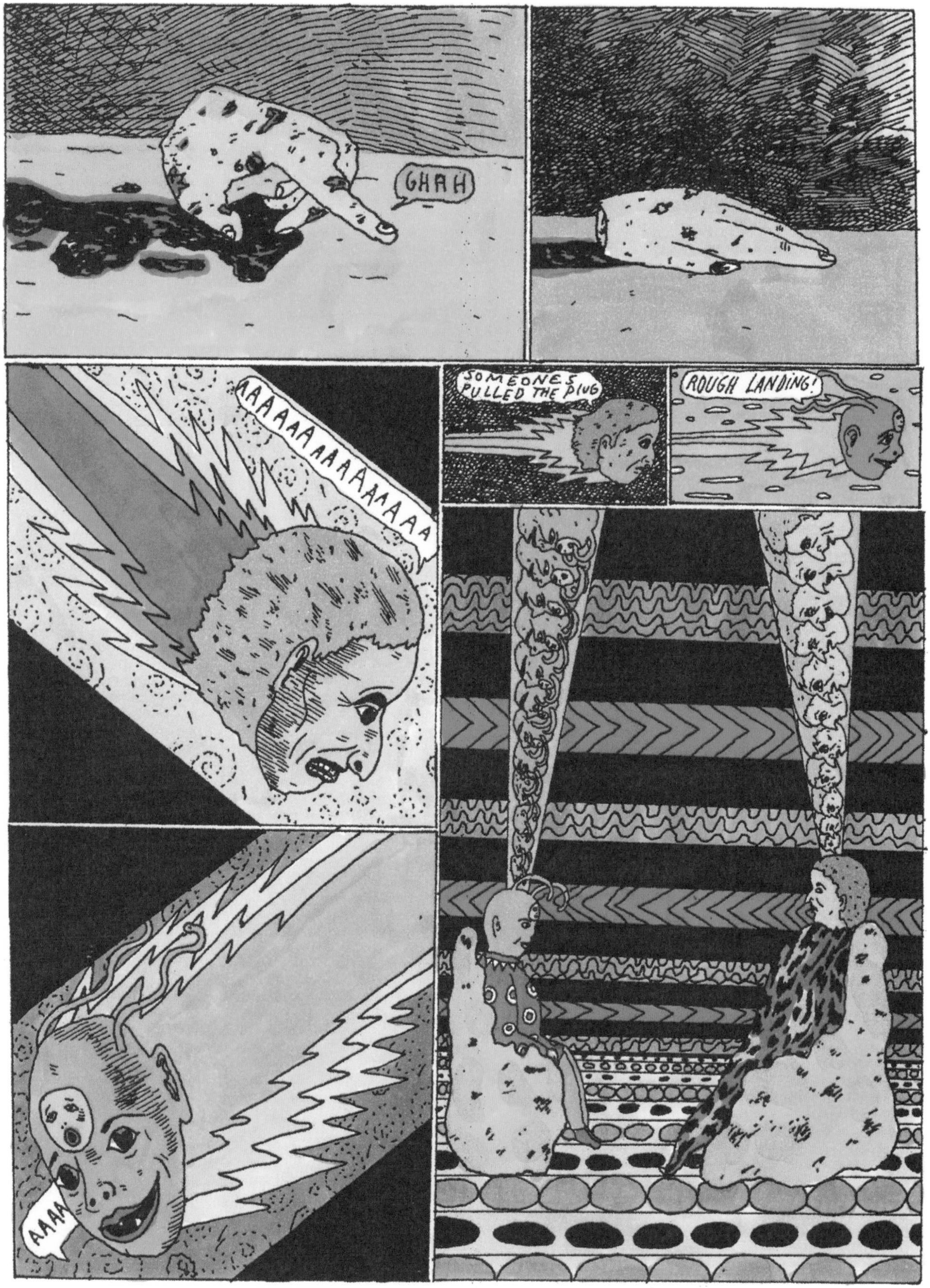
GHAH
AAAAAAAAAAAAAAAAAAA
SOMEONES PULLED THE PLUG
ROUGH LANDING!
AAAA

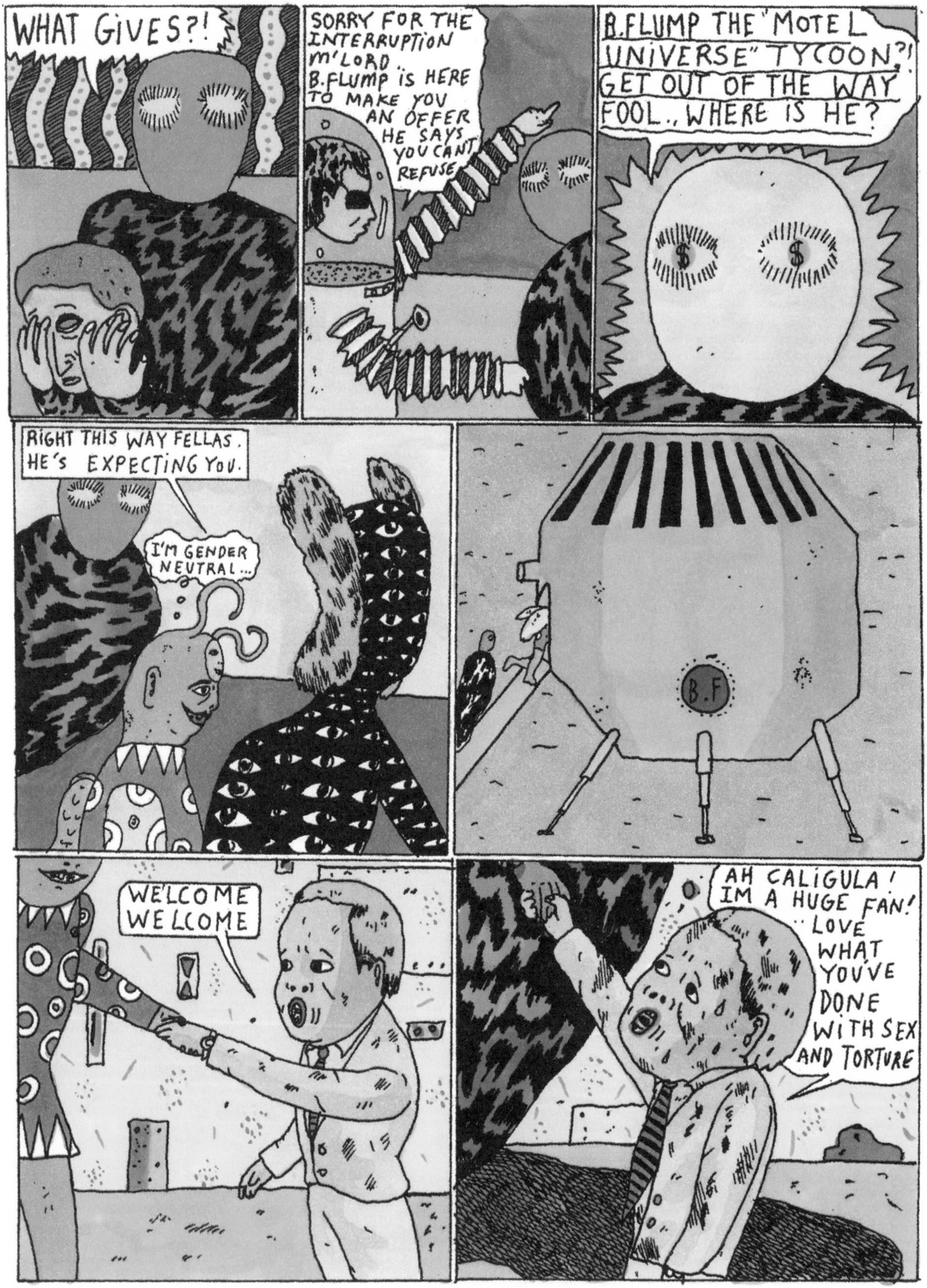
WHAT GIVES?!
SORRY FOR THE INTERRUPTION M'LORD B.FLUMP IS HERE TO MAKE YOU AN OFFER HE SAYS YOU CANT REFUSE
B.FLUMP THE "MOTEL UNIVERSE" TYCOON?! GET OUT OF THE WAY FOOL., WHERE IS HE?
RIGHT THIS WAY FELLAS. HE'S EXPECTING YOU.
I'M GENDER NEUTRAL...
B.F
WELCOME WELCOME
AH CALIGULA! IM A HUGE FAN! ..LOVE WHAT YOU'VE DONE WITH SEX AND TORTURE

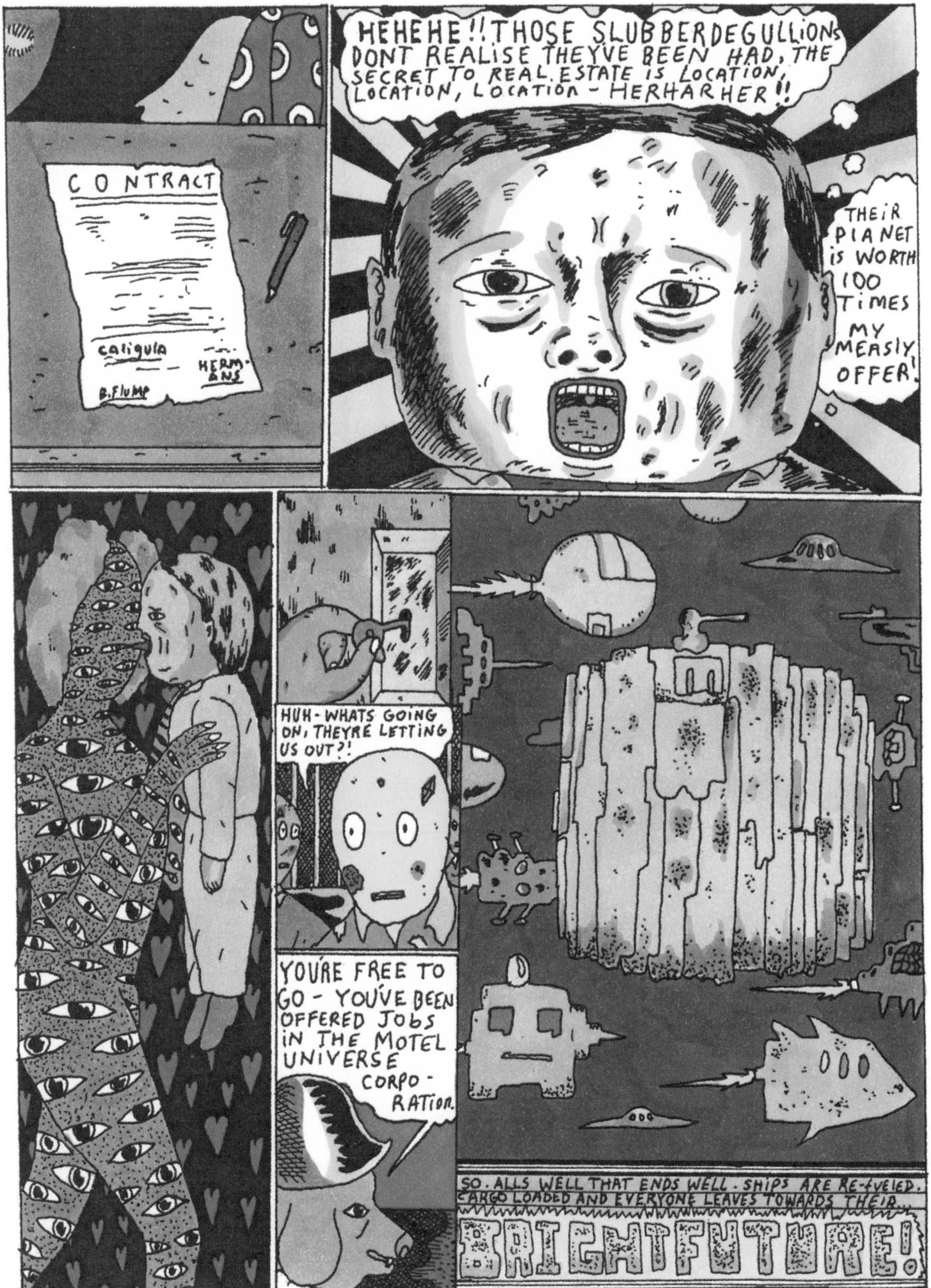
CONTRACT
caligula
HERM-ANS
B.Flump
HEHEHE!! THOSE SLUBBERDEGULLIONS DONT REALISE THEYVE BEEN HAD, THE SECRET TO REAL ESTATE IS LOCATION, LOCATION, LOCATION - HERHARHER!!
THEIR PIANET IS WORTH 100 TIMES MY MEASLY OFFER!
HUH - WHATS GOING ON, THEYRE LETTING US OUT?!
YOU'RE FREE TO GO - YOU'VE BEEN OFFERED JOBS IN THE MOTEL UNIVERSE CORPO-RATION.
SO. ALLS WELL THAT ENDS WELL. SHIPS ARE RE-FUELED. CARGO LOADED AND EVERYONE LEAVES TOWARDS THEIR
BRIGHTFUTURE!

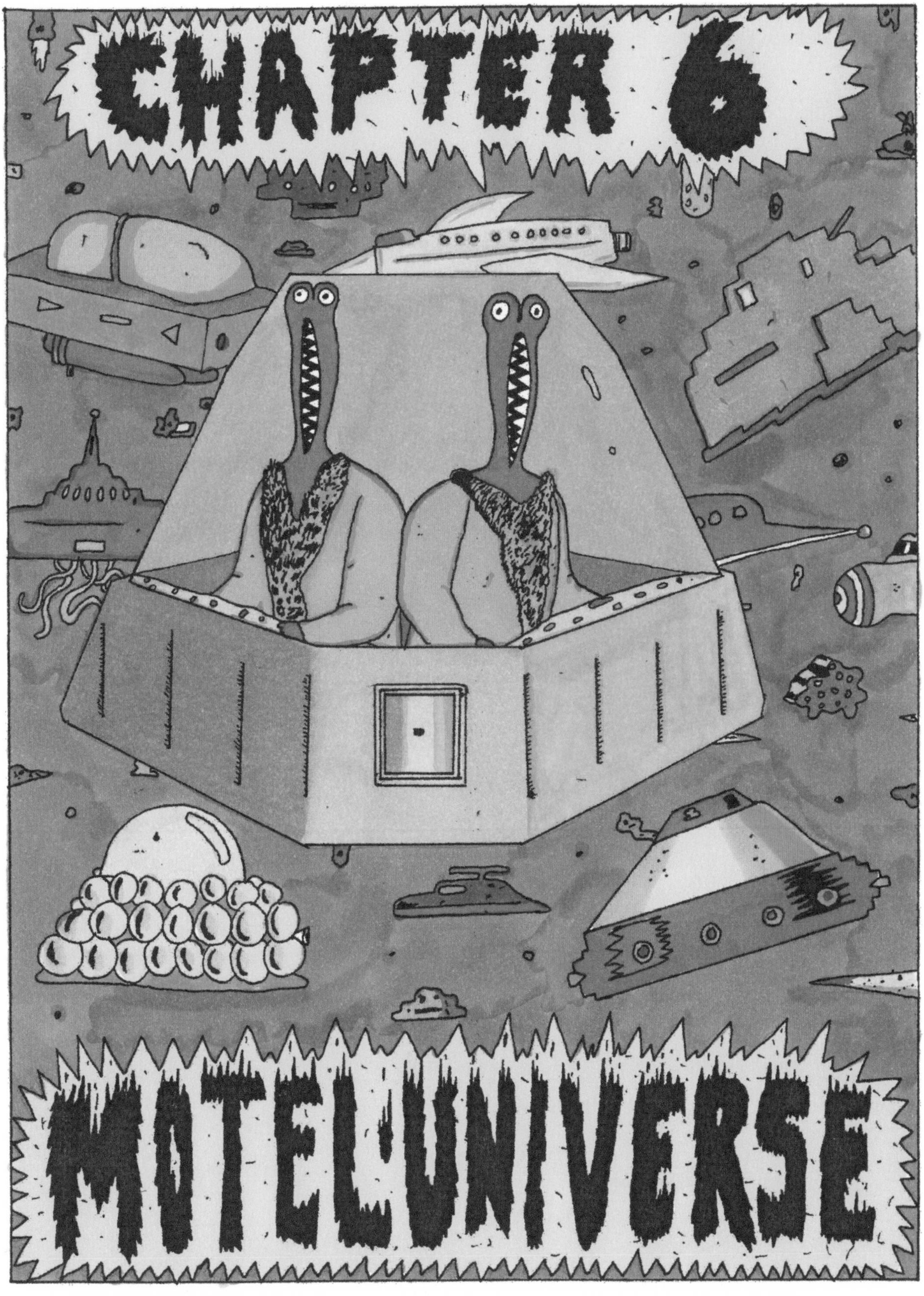
CHAPTER 6
MOTELUNIVERSE

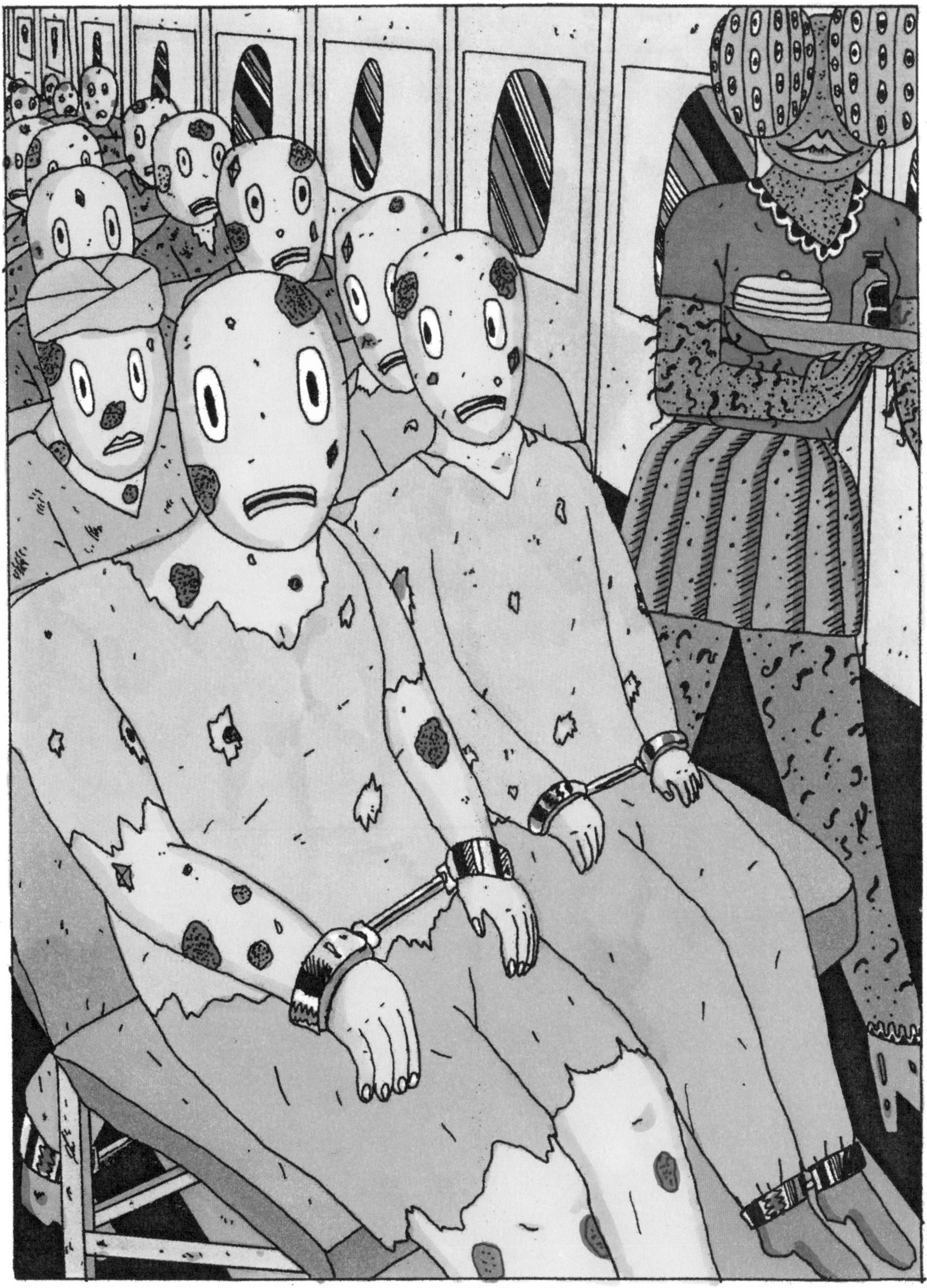

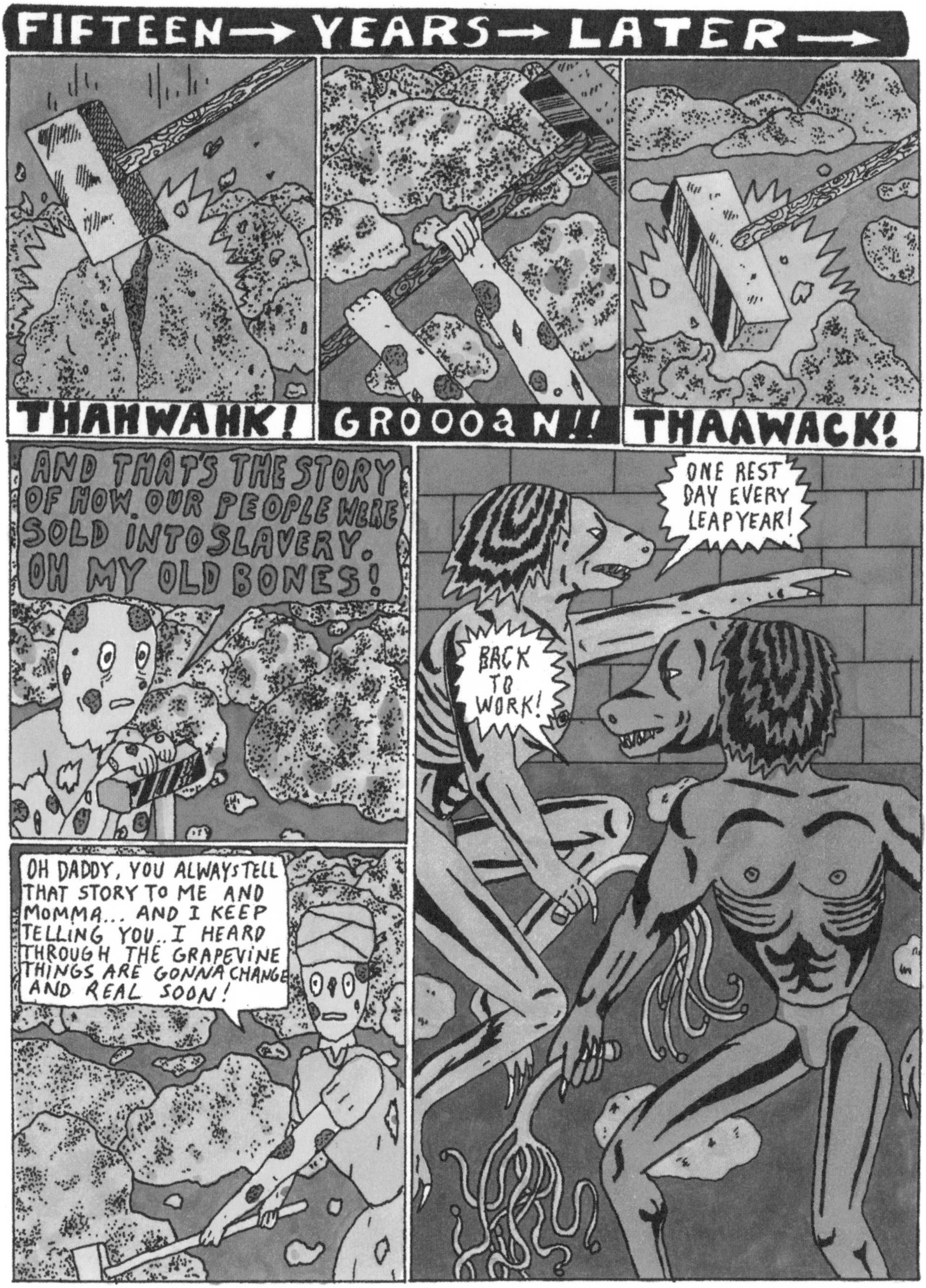
FIFTEEN → YEARS → LATER →
THAHWAHK!
GROOOaN!!
THAAWACK!
AND THAT'S THE STORY OF HOW OUR PEOPLE WERE SOLD INTO SLAVERY. OH MY OLD BONES!
ONE REST DAY EVERY LEAP YEAR!
BACK TO WORK!
OH DADDY, YOU ALWAYS TELL THAT STORY TO ME AND MOMMA... AND I KEEP TELLING YOU.. I HEARD THROUGH THE GRAPEVINE THINGS ARE GONNA CHANGE AND REAL SOON!

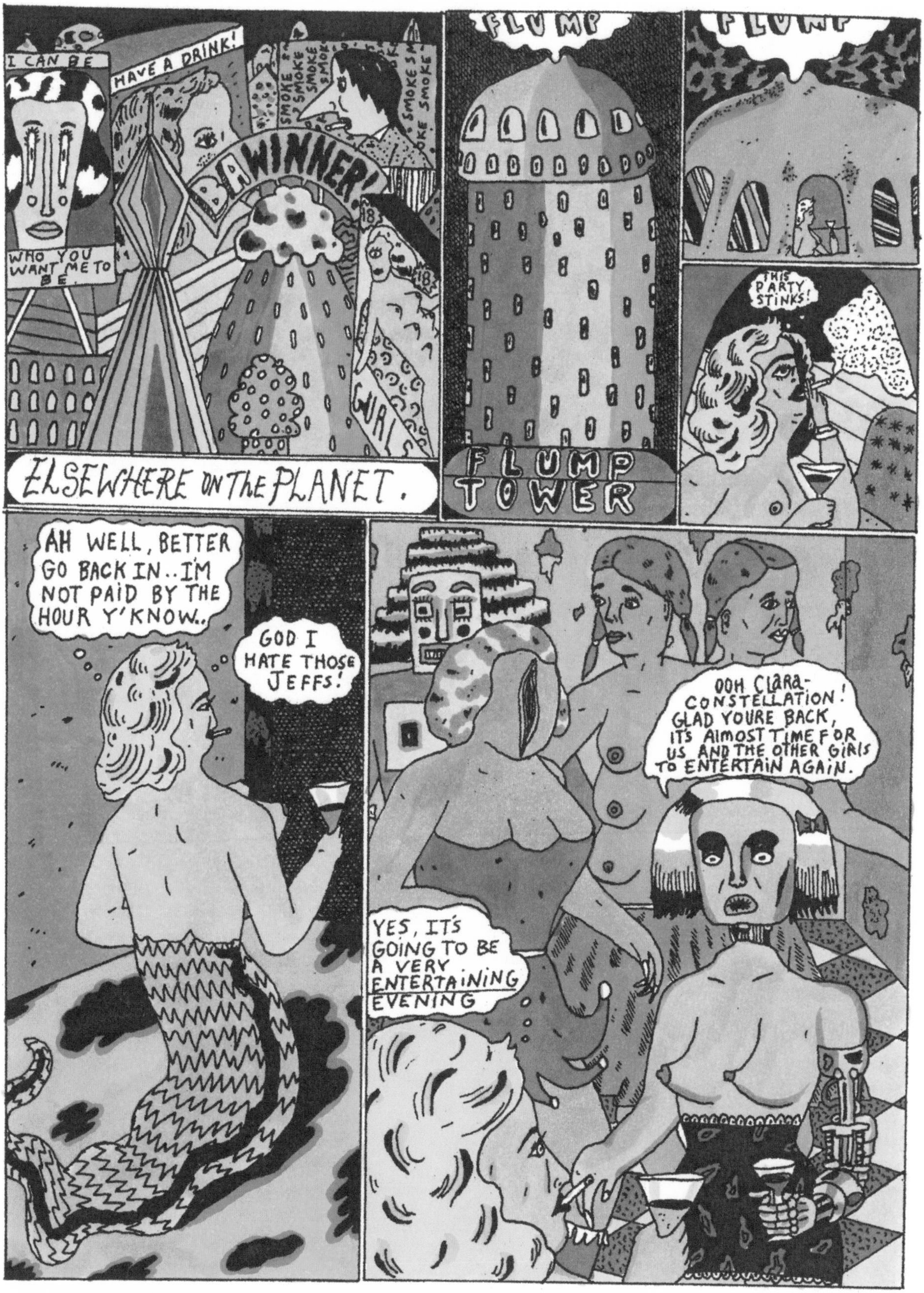

I CAN BE
WHO YOU WANT ME TO BE.
HAVE A DRINK!
SMOKE SMOKE SMOKE
BAWINNER!
18
GIRLS
ELSEWHERE ON THE PLANET.
FLUMP
FLUMP TOWER
FLUMP
THIS PARTY STINKS!
AH WELL, BETTER GO BACK IN.. I'M NOT PAID BY THE HOUR Y'KNOW..
GOD I HATE THOSE JEFFS!
OOH CLARA-CONSTELLATION! GLAD YOURE BACK, ITS ALMOST TIME FOR US AND THE OTHER GIRLS TO ENTERTAIN AGAIN.
YES, IT'S GOING TO BE A VERY ENTERTAINING EVENING

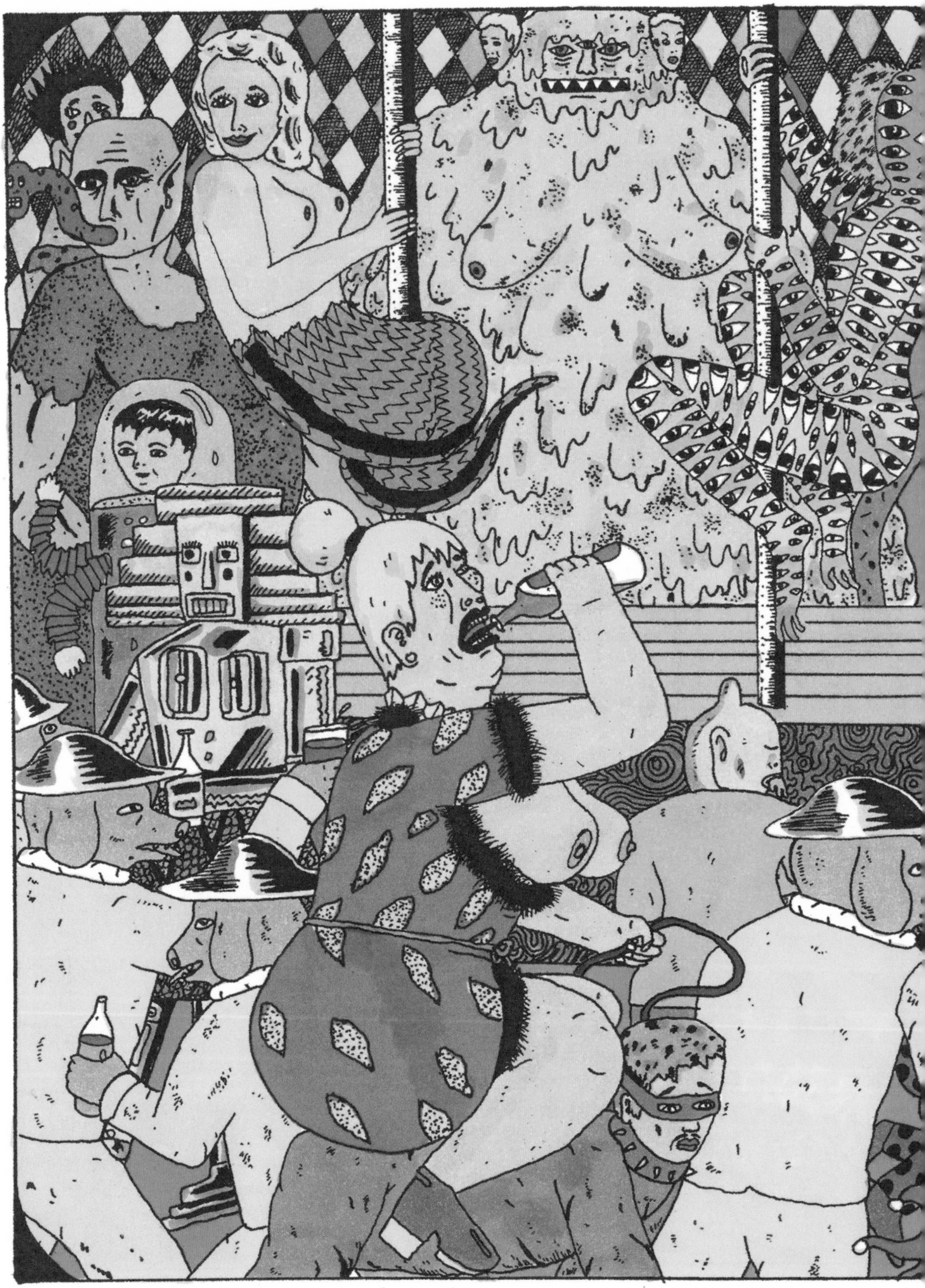

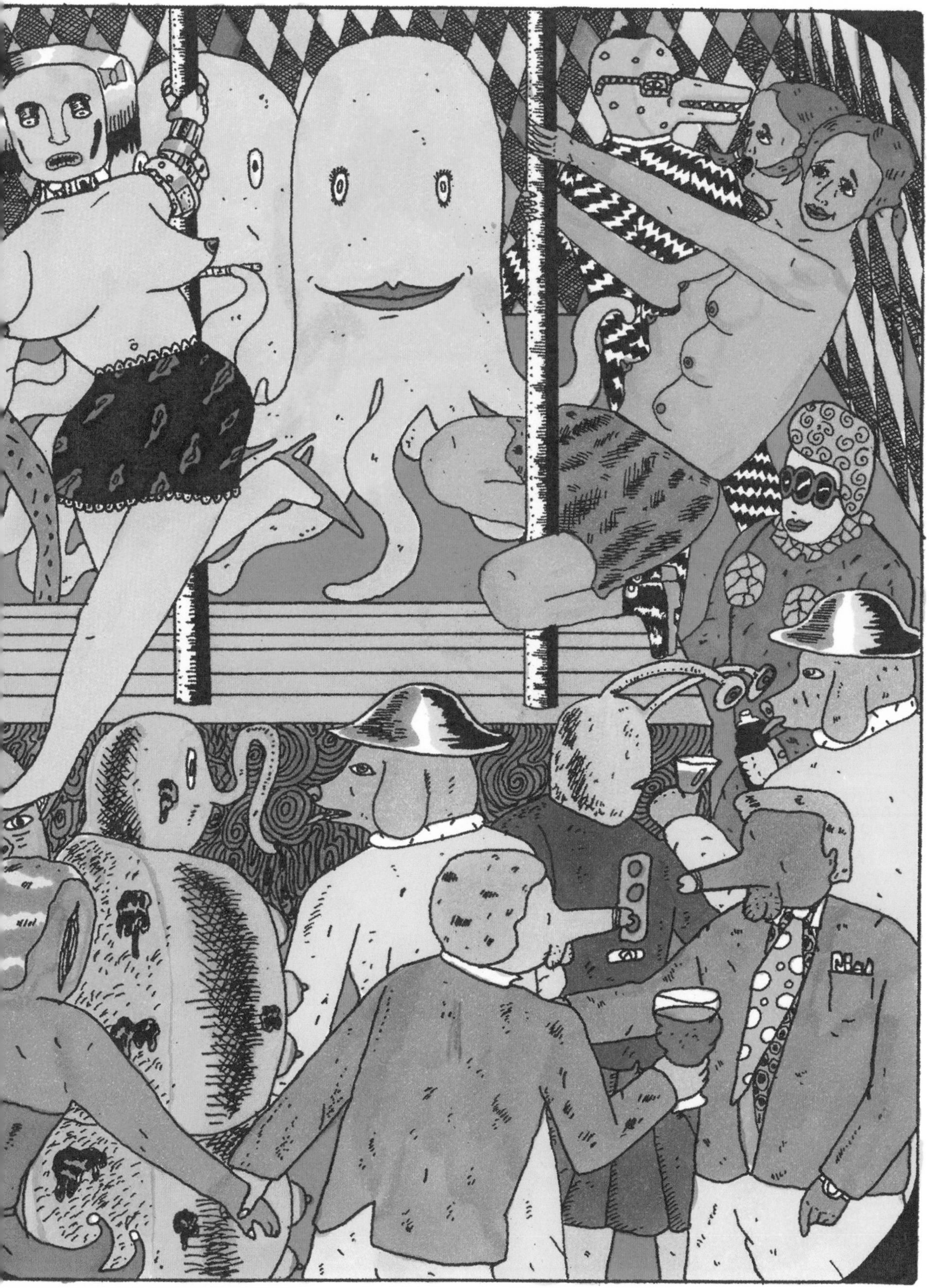

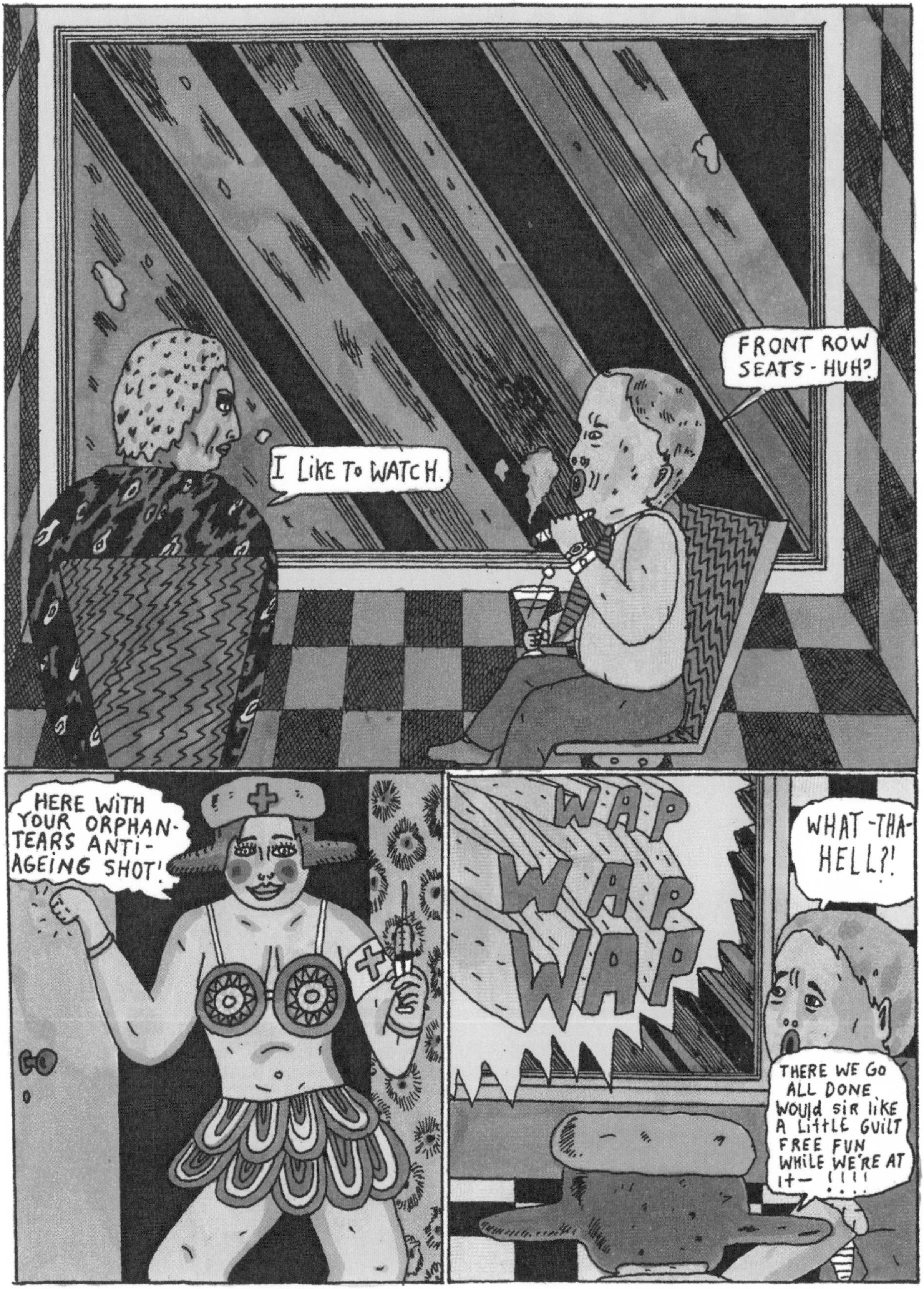
FRONT ROW SEATS - HUH?
I LIKE TO WATCH.
HERE WITH YOUR ORPHAN-TEARS ANTI-AGEING SHOT!
WAP WAP WAP
WHAT-THA-HELL?!
THERE WE GO ALL DONE would sir like A Little GUILT FREE FUN WHILE WE'RE AT it— !!!!

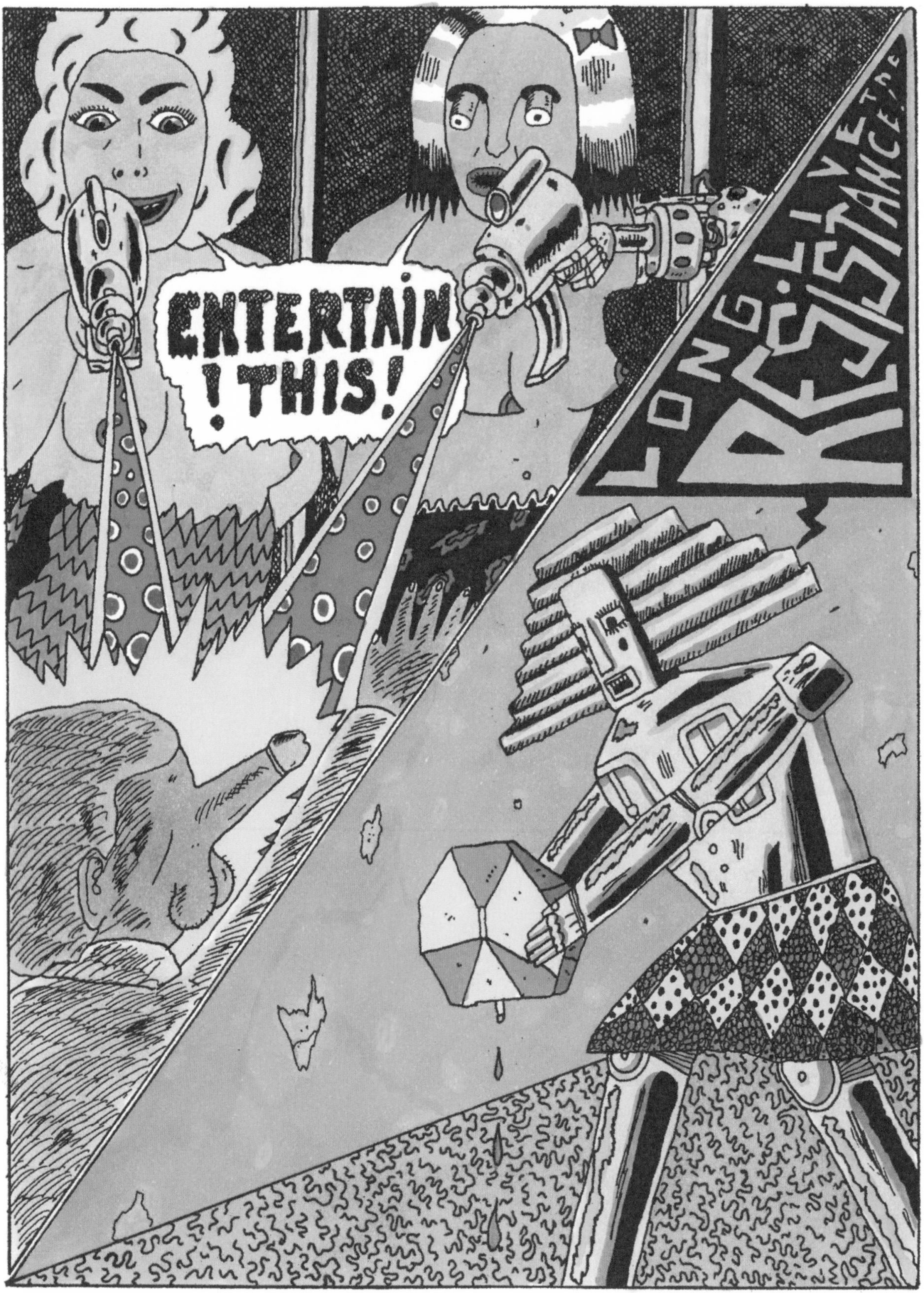
ENTERTAIN !THIS!
LONG LIVE THE RESISTANCE!

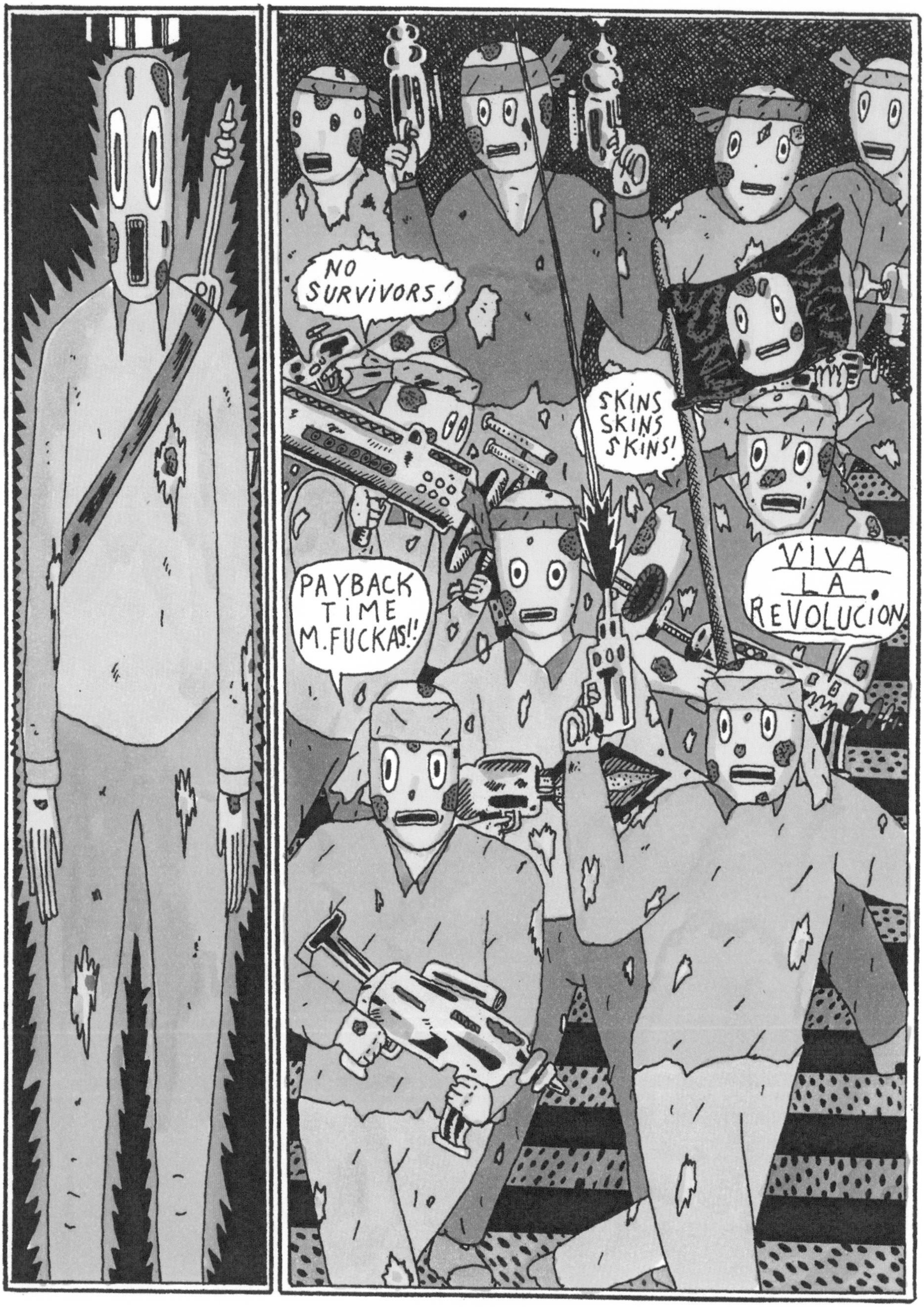
NO SURVIVORS!
SKINS SKINS SKINS!
PAYBACK TIME M.FUCKAS!!
VIVA LA REVOLUCION

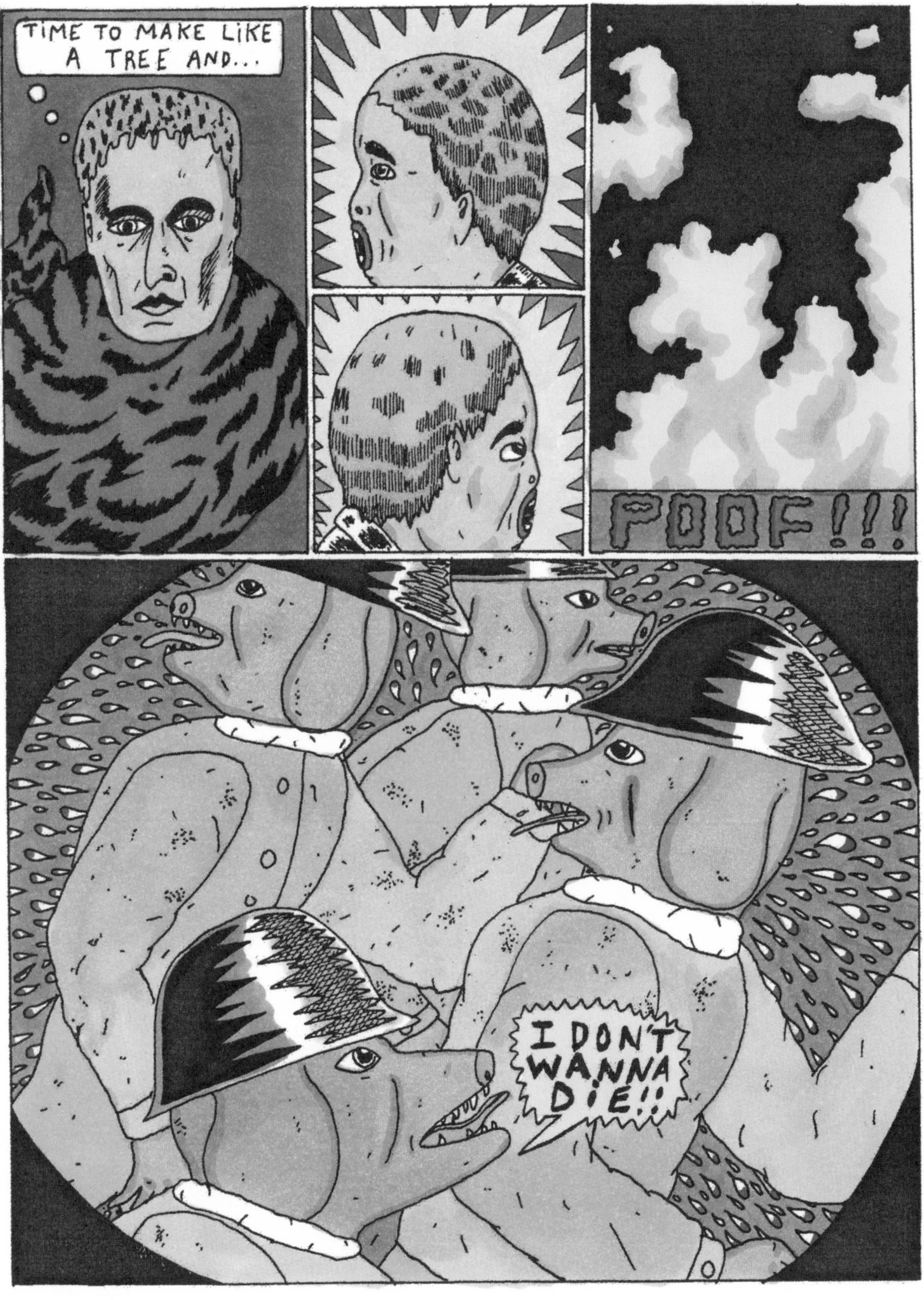
TIME TO MAKE LIKE A TREE AND...
POOF!!!
I DON'T WANNA DIE!!

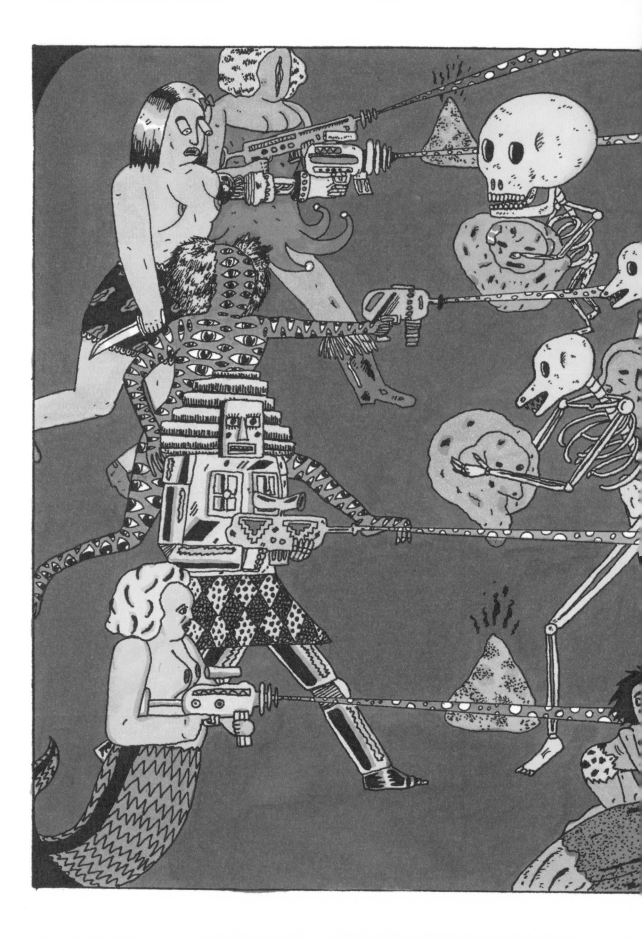

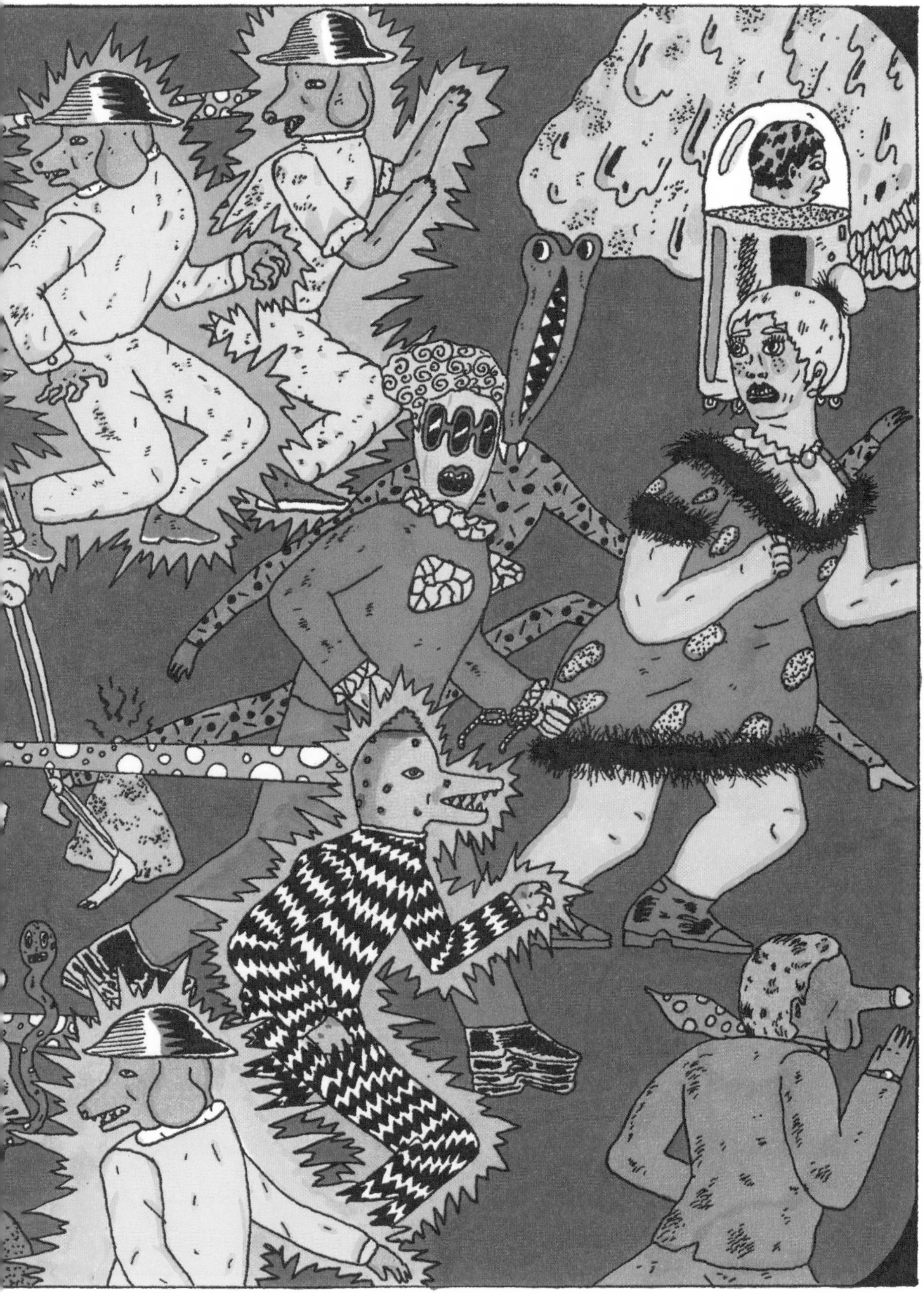

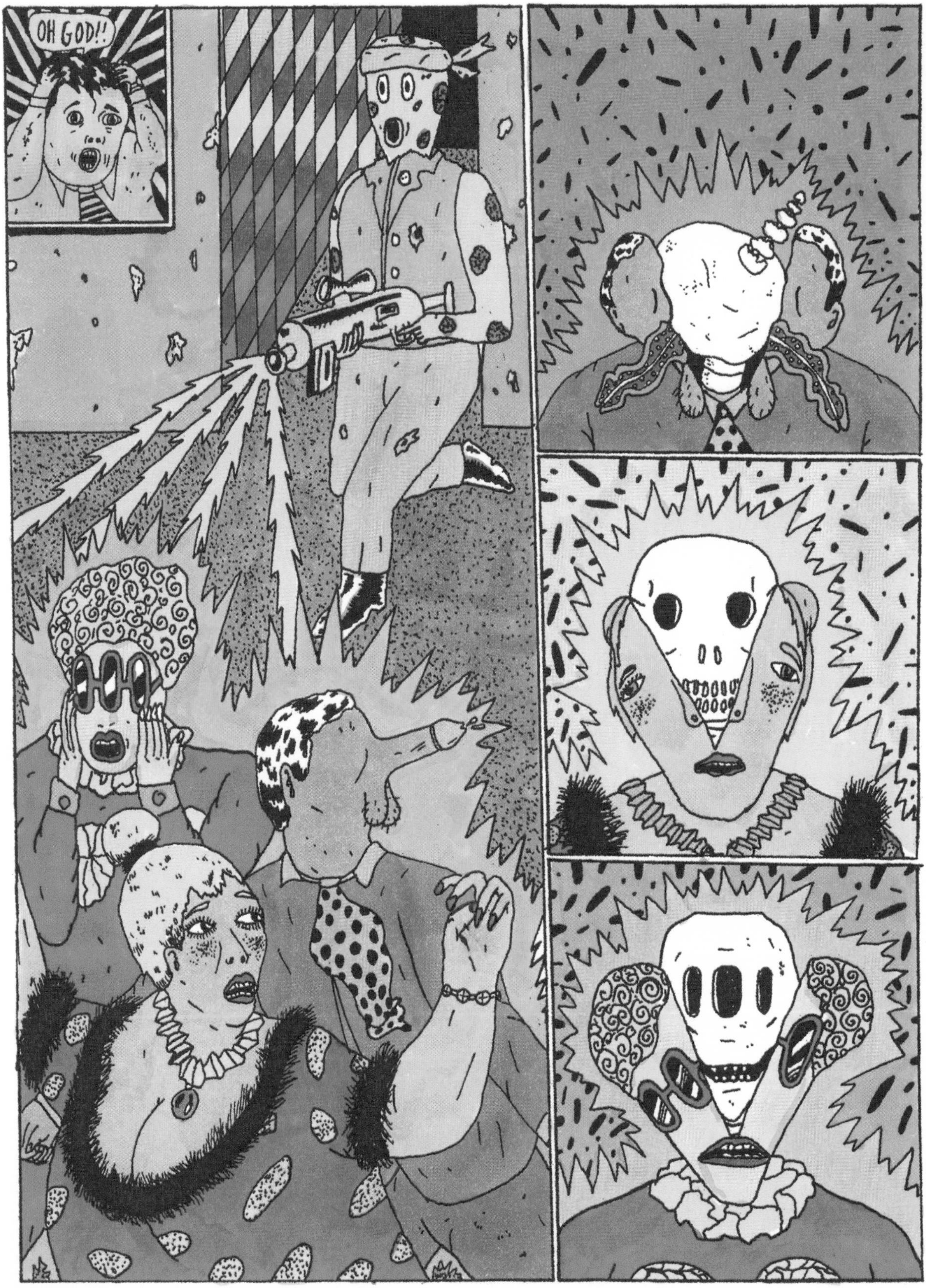
OH GOD!!

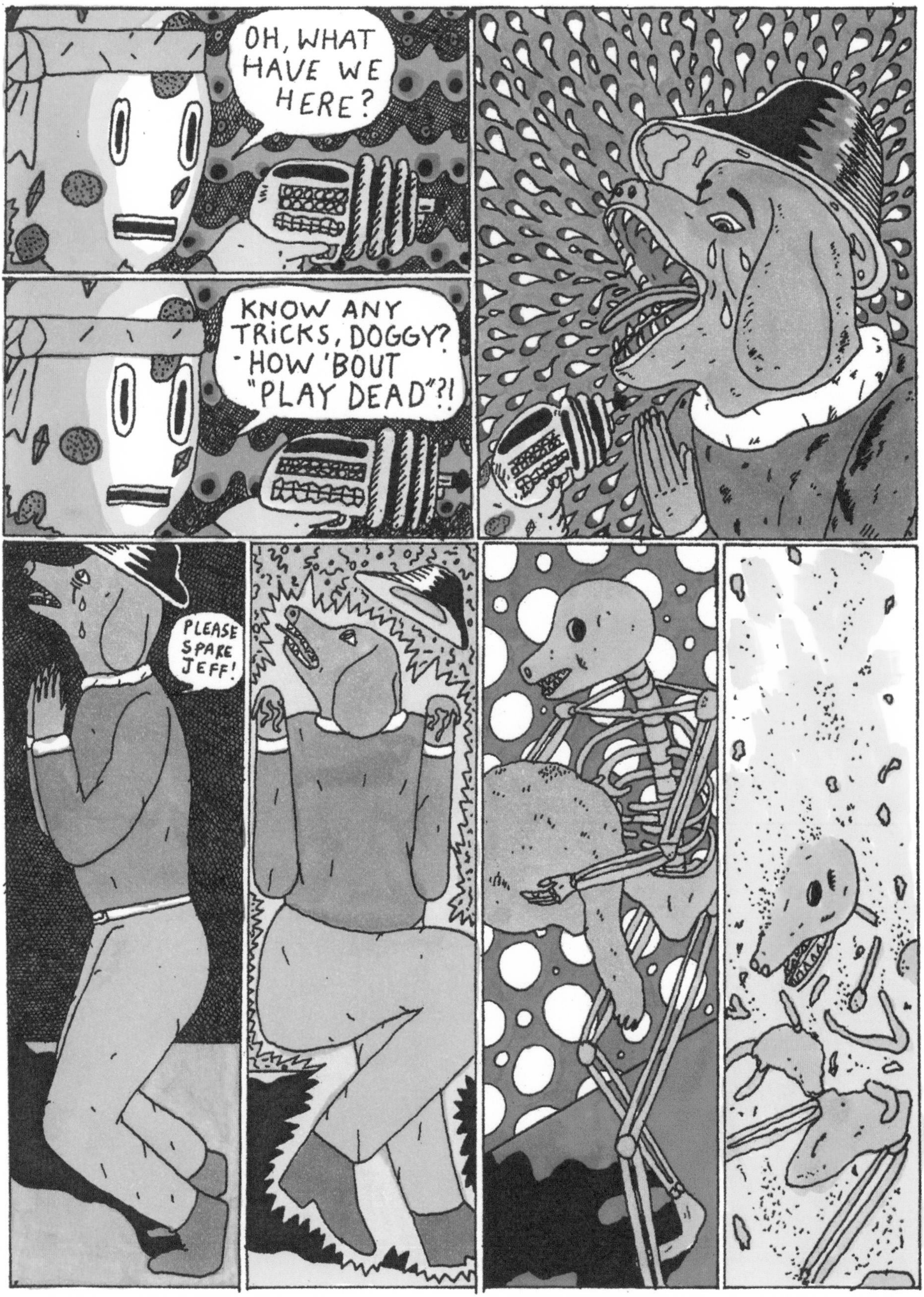
OH, WHAT HAVE WE HERE?
KNOW ANY TRICKS, DOGGY? - HOW 'BOUT "PLAY DEAD"?!
PLEASE SPARE JEFF!

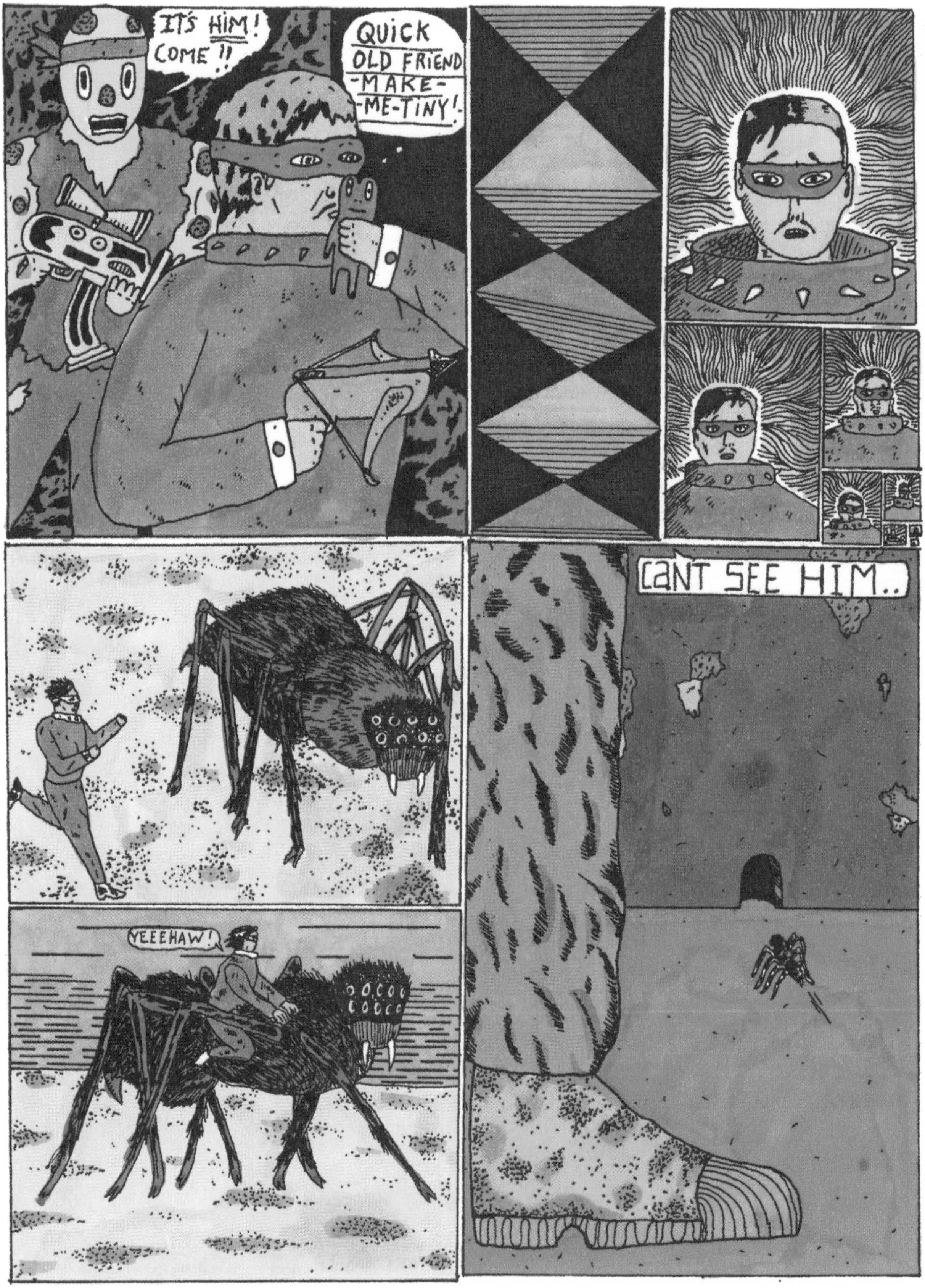

IT'S HIM! COME !!
QUICK OLD FRIEND -MAKE- -ME-TINY!
YEEEHAW!
CANT SEE HIM..

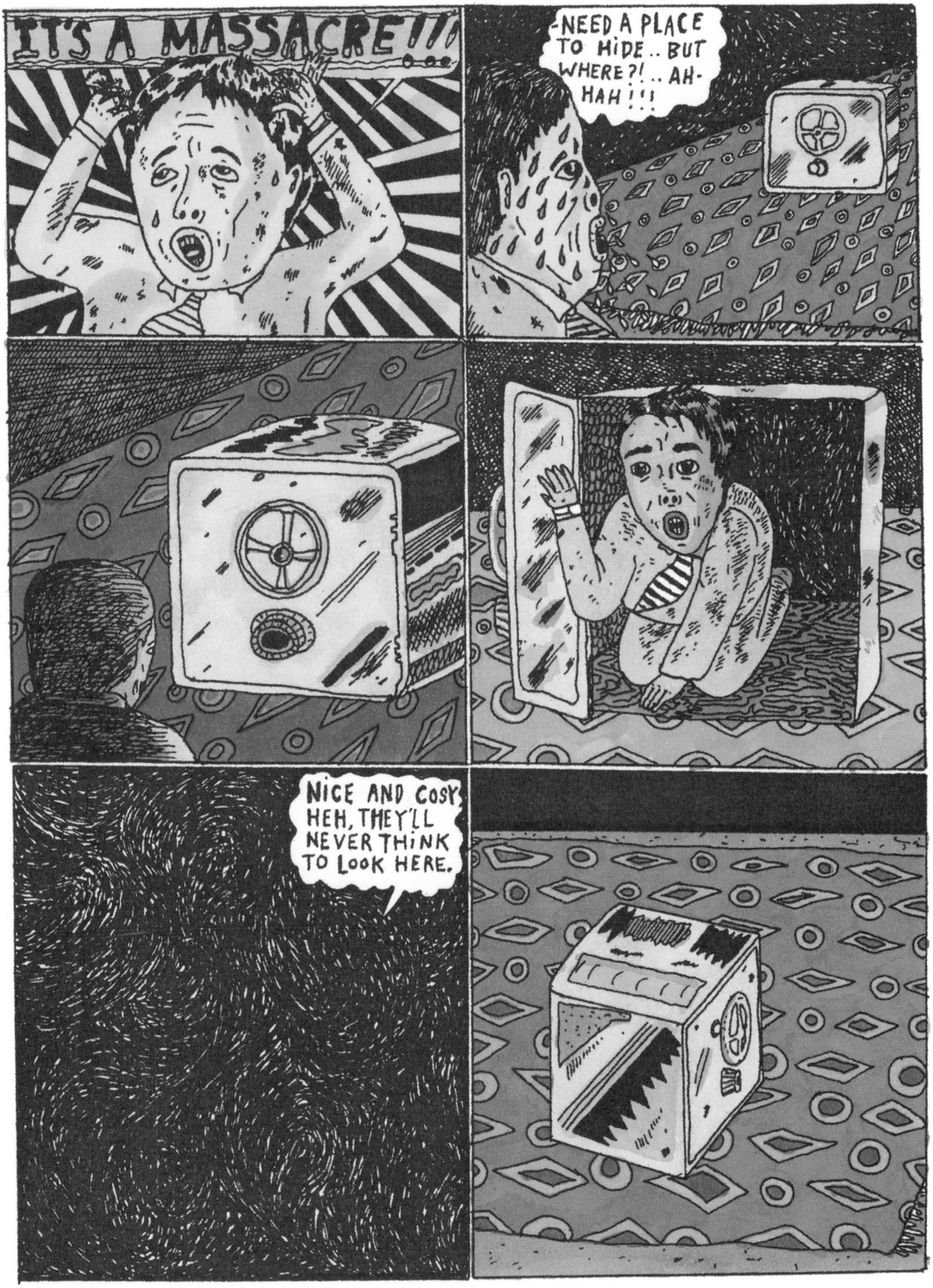
IT'S A MASSACRE!!!
-NEED A PLACE TO HIDE.. BUT WHERE?!.. AH-HAH!!!
NICE AND COSY HEH, THEY'LL NEVER THINK TO LOOK HERE.

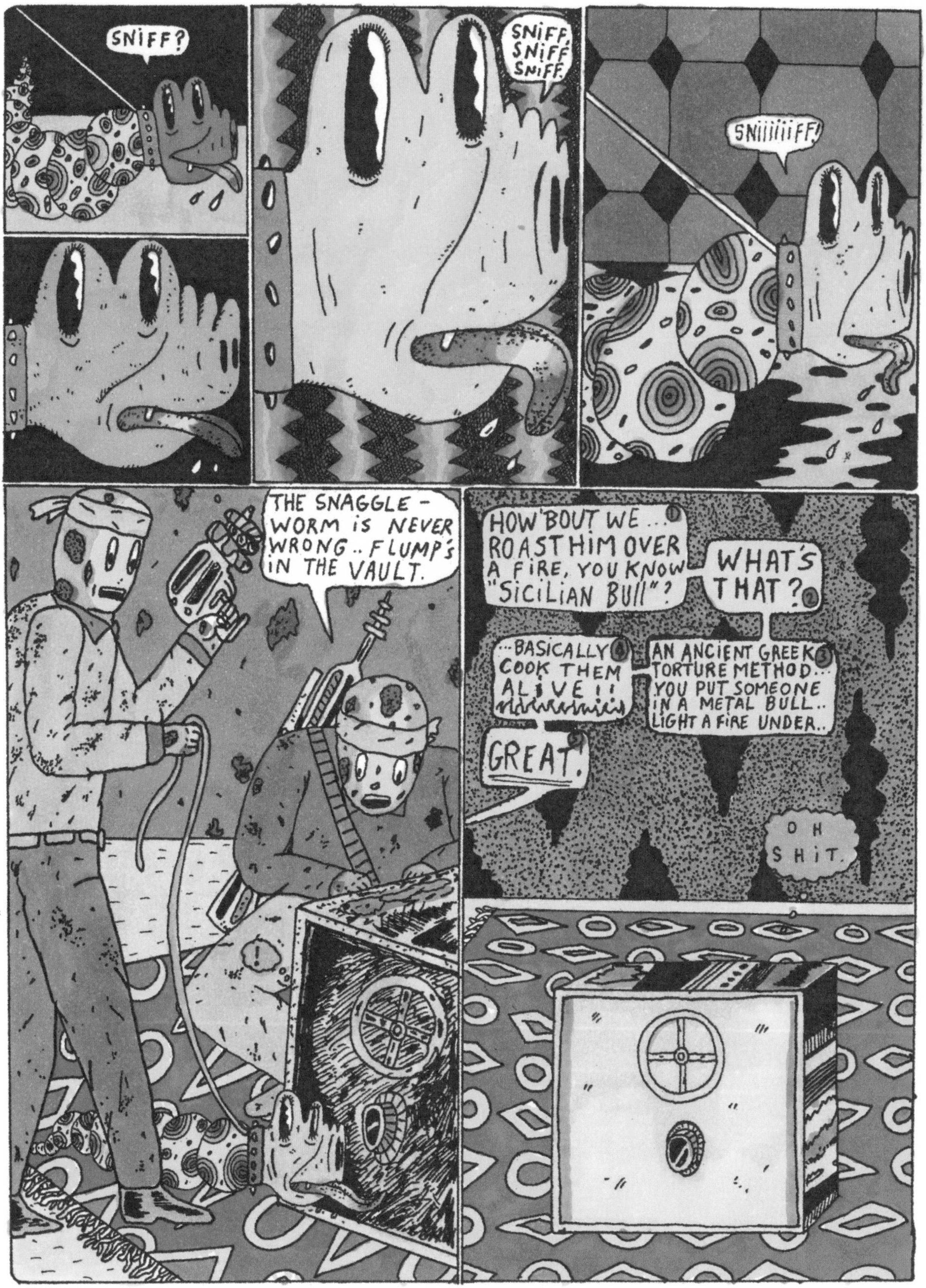
SNIFF?
SNIFF, SNIFF SNIFF.
SNIIIIIIFF!
THE SNAGGLE-WORM IS NEVER WRONG.. FLUMP'S IN THE VAULT.
!
HOW'BOUT WE... ROAST HIM OVER A FIRE, YOU KNOW "SICILIAN BULL"?
WHAT'S THAT?
AN ANCIENT GREEK TORTURE METHOD.. YOU PUT SOMEONE IN A METAL BULL.. LIGHT A FIRE UNDER..
...BASICALLY COOK THEM ALIVE!!
GREAT.
OH SHIT.

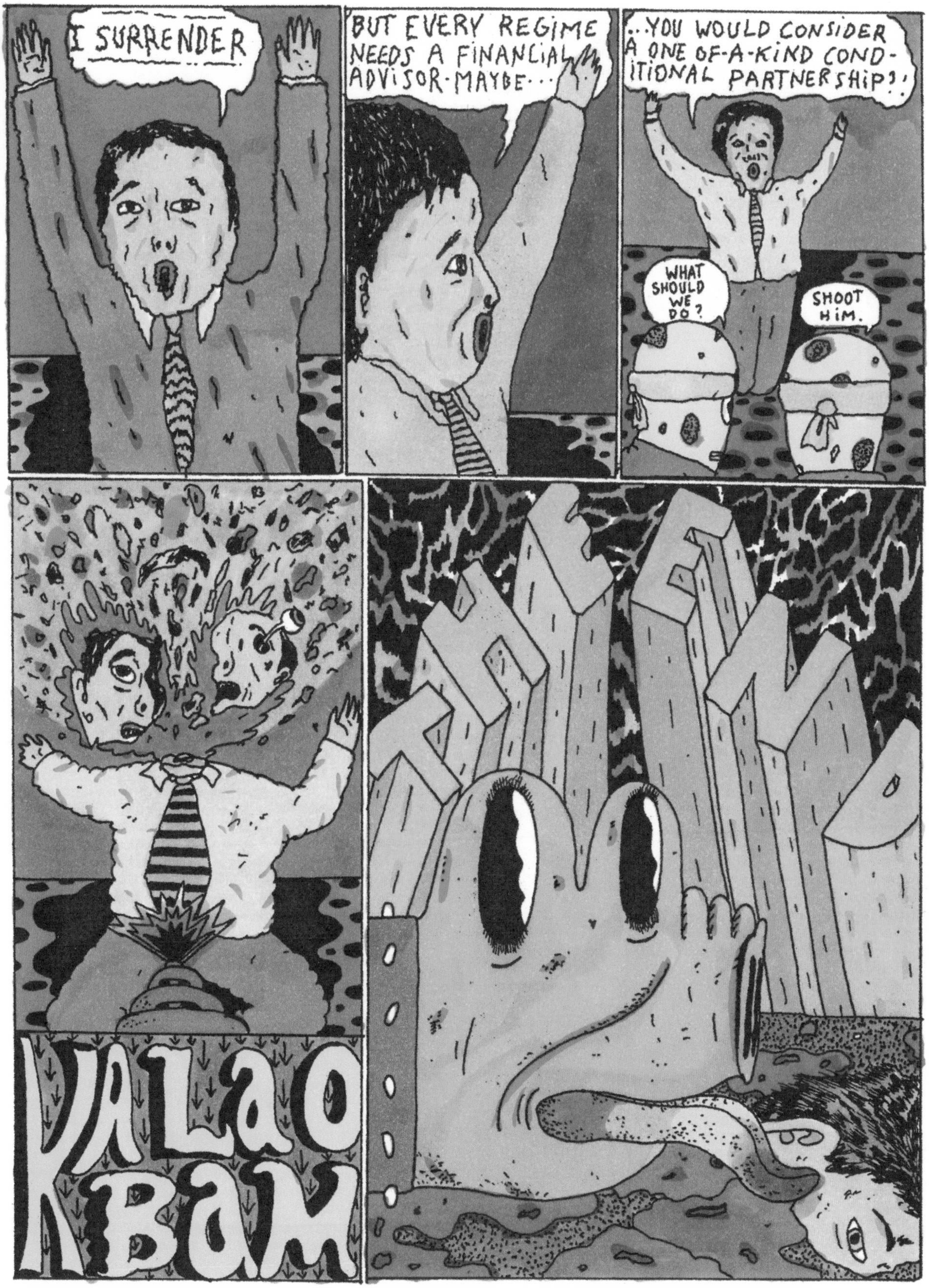
I SURRENDER
BUT EVERY REGIME NEEDS A FINANCIAL ADVISOR·MAYBE···
..YOU WOULD CONSIDER A ONE-OF-A-KIND CONDITIONAL PARTNERSHIP?!
WHAT SHOULD WE DO?
SHOOT HIM.
KALAO
KBAM
THE END

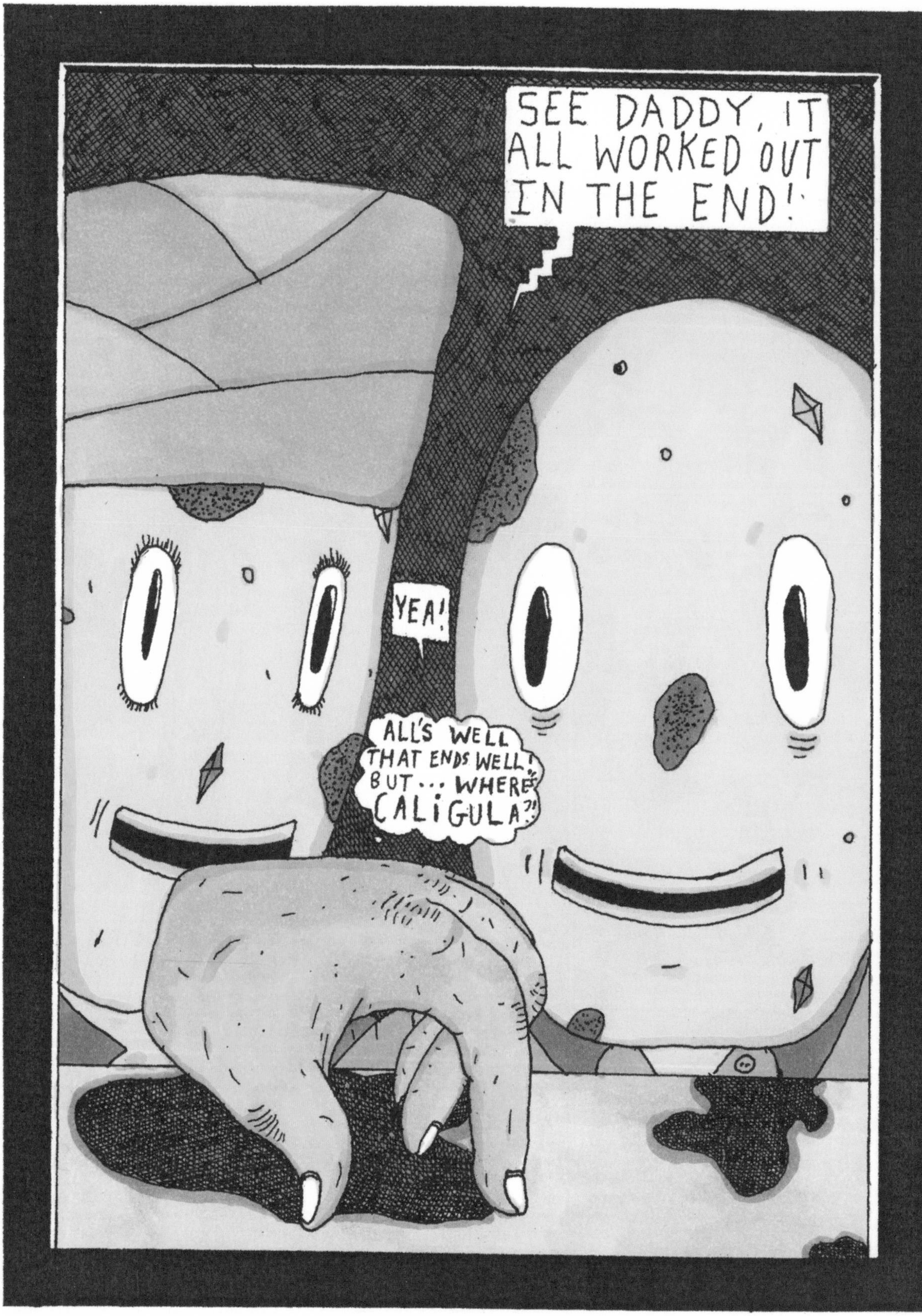
SEE DADDY, IT ALL WORKED OUT IN THE END!
YEA!
ALL'S WELL THAT ENDS WELL! BUT... WHERE'S CALIGULA?!